Penguin Education

The Making of a
1603-1789

A. J. Patrick

A. J. Patrick was born in 1931 and educated at Bishop Vesey's Grammar School, Sutton Coldfield, Hatfield College, Durham, and Birmingham University. He has held a number of teaching posts, and is now Lecturer in History at Aberdeen College of Education.

A History of Britain

The Making of a Nation 1603-1789

A. J. Patrick

Penguin Education

Design: Arthur Lockwood

Illustration research: Nan Russell-Cobb

Penguin Education
Penguin Books Ltd,
Harmondsworth, Middlesex, England
Penguin Books Inc, 7110 Ambassador Road, Baltimore, Md 21207, U.S.A.
Penguin Books Australia Ltd, Ringwood, Victoria, Australia
Penguin Books Canada Ltd, 41 Steelcase Road West, Markham, Ontario, Canada
Penguin Books (N.Z.) Ltd, 182–190 Wairau Road, Auckland 10, New Zealand

First published 1967
Reprinted 1968, 1969, 1970
Revised edition 1971
Reprinted 1972, 1973, 1975
Copyright © A. J. Patrick, 1967, 1971

Printed in Great Britain by Compton Printing Ltd, Aylesbury
Set in Lumitype Plantin

Contents

Chapter 1
The reign of James I 1603-25

The new age

In 1603, most Englishmen must have felt that a new age had dawned. Queen Elizabeth, who had ruled for forty-five years, was dead and in her place England had a king. He was Elizabeth's cousin, a man of thirty-seven, who had been King of Scotland ever since he was a baby. He was the son of Mary Queen of Scots, about whom you read in the last volume. His name was James Stuart, and with his accession the rule of the Tudor family ended, and that of the Stuarts began. If you look at the family tree on page 17, you will see how he came to inherit the throne.

The problems

Neither James I nor his son Charles, who succeeded him in 1625, found England an easy country to govern. Two great problems dominated their reigns. First, many Englishmen wished to change the form of the country's religion, while James and Charles were both broadly satisfied with the Church of England, whose foundation is described in *A History of Britain* SH2. The critics of the Church were called Puritans, and you will read of their beliefs later.

The second problem struck at the very roots of the whole system of government. In the past kings and queens had relied mostly on the landowners to help them govern the country. Thus, most of the Council were landowners, so were the members of the House of Lords and many of the members of the House of Commons. Even the Justices of the Peace were landowners. This system had worked well, but by 1603 it was out of date because it ignored the growing wealth and power of the merchants and industrialists. They wanted more say in how their country should be governed now that England was a trading nation. Some of them, therefore, became members of the House of Commons, and began to demand more power for this assembly. Neither James nor Charles was willing to grant it. In the next two chapters we shall see, among other things, how they dealt with the Puritans in the Church and the merchants, many of whom were also Puritans, in the Commons.

Religion in 1603

Today we take it for granted that our religious beliefs are not the business of the government. There is no law laying down what we have to believe, and we are free to practise whatever religion we choose, or even none at all. This was not so at the beginning of the seventeenth century – quite the opposite, in fact. Most people thought that the government of a country was given its power by God and thus believed

Portrait of James I, in robes of State, painted in 1625 when he was 59 years old. The garter on his left leg is the insignia of the Knights of the Garter. James rarely looked as splendid as this, as he was very careless with his clothes and hated elaborate costumes.

The main Catholic and Protestant powers in Europe in 1610. Spain and France were the Catholic strongholds: Holland and Britain the most important Protestant countries. Germany consisted of a huge number of semi-independent countries, some Catholic, some Protestant.

that the government ought to settle the form of religion for its people. If some of its subjects refused to worship as they were told, then they had to expect to be punished. This did not seem wrong to people; they took it for granted, just as we take it for granted that everybody has got to go to school.

Laws on religion

By 1603 the Reformation had taken place and Europe was split into Catholic and Protestant countries in the way shown on the map. England was, of course, a Protestant country, with a church of its own of which the King was head, with bishops to help him. Roman Catholics were forbidden to hold services of their own, and everybody was made by law to attend Church of England services every Sunday. Indeed, if anyone failed to go to church, he could be fined a shilling – more than a day's pay for a labourer – for every Sunday he missed. Moreover, Catholic priests were forbidden to enter the country on pain of death. In spite of these laws, the Roman Catholic religion survived in England, especially among those rich enough to pay their fines each week. Sometimes, as you read in *A History of Britain* SH2, they would have special hiding places made in their houses so that their priests, who went from house to house to hold services in secret, would not be found if the building were searched while they were there. Some of these survive up to the present day.

In their lifetimes these two would never have been found side by side. *Left:* a bishop, complete with his elaborate vestments and prayer book. *Right:* 'Praise God Barebones' himself, in sober, simple dress.

The Puritans

The Puritans were the people who hated the Catholics most. Typical of them was a London merchant, named 'Praise God' Barebones. He was tall and thin, with rather a severe face. He believed that Roman Catholicism was not just mistaken, but was an evil thing, and he could not really trust the Church of England as long as it used Papist ceremonies like confirmation, special clothes for priests and bowing at the name of Christ in the service. In fact, he did not really like a set service at all. He preferred to meet with a few of his friends and hold an informal prayer meeting, where one of them, who knew a lot about the Bible, might preach for anything up to five hours. This was much more than many Anglican parsons could do. Nor were the Puritan sermons dull. Once when 'Praise God' himself was preaching in 1641, he 'yelped so loud with an horrid exclamation, crying divers times, as was audibly heard, "Hell and Damnation"', that a crowd collected outside his house! Nor did 'Praise God' like bishops, believing that each congregation should govern itself. His life had few pleasures. He worked hard for six days a week, and thought that success in his trade was a sign of God's blessing. On Sunday he devoted all his time to his religion, either praying or reading the Bible. He thought any other recreation on Sunday was sinful. He was quite sure that his ideas were right. Indeed, he believed that he and a few others who thought like him had been specially chosen by God to be saved, and that all those who disagreed with him would burn for ever in Hell fire.

As we have already pointed out, there were many Puritans in 1603. Not all of them went as far as did Barebones, but they wanted many reforms in the Church of England. What was more, they thought they might be able to get what they wanted, for James I had been King of Scotland before he came to rule England, and Scotland's church was more Puritan than the Church of England. They therefore presented a petition to the King, asking him to introduce changes in the Church of England. James agreed to meet them at Hampton Court in 1604 to discuss Church reform. The Puritans were very pleased at this, for the fact that James had agreed to discuss the state of the Church with them seemed a sort of victory, as it showed he thought all was not well.

The Hampton Court Conference   1604

But the Puritans were doomed to disappointment. In his early years James had been bullied and insulted by the Elders of the Scottish Church. His tutor, George Buchanan, had often beaten him, and James was so frightened of him that years later he used to tremble at the sight of one of his courtiers who reminded him of his old teacher. As late as 1596 another minister, Andrew Melville, had shouted James down, calling him 'God's silly vassal' in front of the whole court. Memories like this came crowding into James's mind when he faced the Puritans. In Scotland he had had to put up with it, but in England, where the Puritans had no real power, there was no reason why he should. Thus, when the conference started, James was quite prepared for a quarrel.

In fact, all went quite well until one of the Puritans happened to mention the word 'presbytery'. A presbytery was a committee of laymen who advised Puritan clergy. In Scotland they were very powerful, and James took fright as soon as he heard the word. He shouted out that presbyteries agreed about as well with a monarchy 'as God and the Devil. Then Tom and Dick shall meet and at their pleasure censure me and my council. When I mean to live under a presbytery, I will go into Scotland again, but while I am in England I will have bishops to govern the Church.' He wound up by declaring that he would make the Puritans conform, or would 'harry them out of this land, or else do worse'. He was determined that all the ministers of the Church should accept the rule of bishops and the *Book of Common Prayer*. In all, about ninety clergymen were turned out of their livings because they refused. It was not easy to find replacements. Some Puritans, discouraged, left the country, going either to Holland or America to find freedom to worship as they pleased. Others stayed in England, continuing to hold their own meetings, and some got themselves into Parliament to try to alter the laws governing the Church. One good result of the meeting was the publication of the Authorized Version of the Bible in 1611.

The Gunpowder Plot   1605

But the year after the conference, the Puritans were forgotten in all the

A print of Westminster. Only Westminster Hall is still recognizable. The Parliament house was burned down in 1834, and Westminster Abbey has been much altered.

The Commons in session, 1624. The building seems very uncomfortable and overcrowded. The Speaker sits in the raised chair, with the clerks of the House at the table below him. They merely recorded the decisions of the House and did not note down what was said in debate.

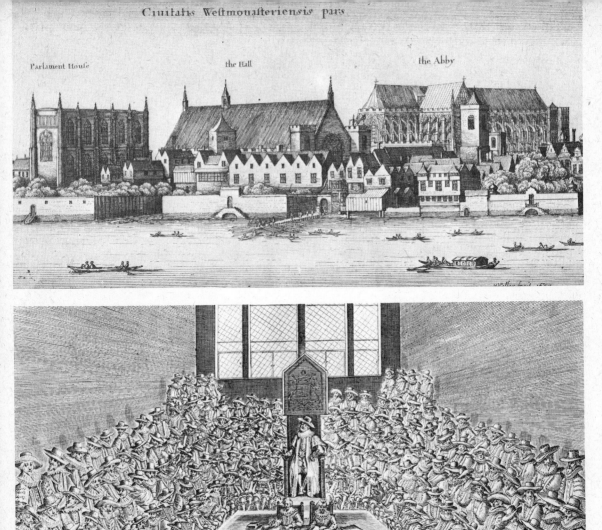

Ciuitatis Westmonasteriensis pars

Parlament House   the Hall   the Abby

A Dutch engraving of the Gunpowder Plotters. None of them is likely to be a good portrait as it is very unlikely that the engraver ever saw any of them.

excitement and horror of the Gunpowder Plot. This plot began because the Catholics, who had supported James's claim to the English throne, expected some help from him in return. They got none. Now he was King of England he had, he said 'No need of the Papists'. This made some Catholics very angry, and two of them, Thomas Percy and Robert Catesby, decided to destroy the King and Parliament by blowing them up at the State Opening.

By May 1604 three others, including Guy Fawkes, had been brought into the scheme. The plotters rented a house near Parliament and began to tunnel from the cellar towards the House of Lords, where the State Opening would take place. The work was desperately hard and time was short. By March 1605, in spite of bringing in other people, they were still a long way from the Lords' chamber. Then they found that the house next to theirs had a cellar to let which ran under the House of Lords. They at once took it, heaped into it thirty-six barrels of gunpowder and some iron bars and covered the whole lot up with firewood. Then they had to wait until Parliament met and, at the right moment, apply a match.

The discovery of the plot

But some of the conspirators began to have second thoughts. There were Catholics in the House of Lords, and it seemed wrong that they should die with the rest. One of the plotters felt so strongly about this that he wrote a letter, reproduced on page 17, to a Catholic, Lord Monteagle, warning him not to attend Parliament. Monteagle took the letter to the Council, who suspected that it might mean that there was to be an explosion sometime during Parliament's sitting. Not that they were sure. They thought it quite likely that the whole thing was a hoax. For the time being, therefore, they did nothing.

Two days before Parliament was due to meet, James came to London and was shown the letter. Now at best James was always very anxious

One of James I's guards. The 'I.R.' on his tunic stands for Iacobus Rex – Latin for King James. The weapon in his left hand is a halberd.

A Dutch engraving of the execution of the Gunpowder Plotters. *Foreground:* the plotters are being drawn on sledges to the scaffold, *centre,* where others are being hanged, drawn and quartered. The engraver has made no attempt to make the picture accurate. The houses, for instance, are typical of those of a Dutch town, but nothing like English houses.

about his own safety. A number of his ancestors, including his father and mother, had died violent deaths and he feared that the same thing might happen to him. This made him very nervous of strangers, following them about with his eyes as long as they were in the room. His clothes were specially padded to be dagger-proof and he would faint with fear if a sword was drawn in his presence. When he read Monteagle's letter all his worst fears seemed confirmed. His father's palace had been blown up. He decided that a thorough search must be made of the cellars and at eleven o'clock that night, 4 November, the gunpowder was discovered and Fawkes, who was on guard, was arrested. The game was up.

Under torture Fawkes told all that he knew, and a band of men went to arrest the conspirators who had fled to Holmbeach House in Worcestershire. They were brought to London, tried for high treason, found guilty, and hanged, drawn and quartered. The only result of the plot was to make the Catholics even more unpopular. Parliament passed

very strict laws against them, but these laws were never enforced all over the country or for long at a time.

James and Spain

You might have expected that James himself would never forgive the Catholics for attempting to blow him up, but he tried his best to see that they were not treated too badly. This was partly because he planned that his son Charles should marry a Spanish princess. His daughter, Elizabeth, had married a Protestant prince from Germany, and he thought it would be a good thing if his son married someone of the Catholic faith. In this way, he felt he might be able to do something to bring the two religions closer together. At all events, James did his best to make a good impression on the Spanish. He had Sir Walter Raleigh executed on a charge of high treason because the Spanish hated him, and tried to make things easier for English Catholics. His efforts did him little good. The English Parliament had no use for James's schemes. They wanted his son to marry a Protestant, and would have been glad to see England at war with Spain. In 1621 they told James what they thought.

James and Parliament

Parliament's advice made James furious. They had already made difficulties more than once over granting him sufficient funds. They failed to realize that the government cost more to run, and thought

This Dutch engraving of London shows the variety and quantity of traffic carried on the river in the early seventeenth century. The Tower of London dominates the opposite bank of the river.

14

James extravagant. Now they were seeking to tell him how to conduct his foreign policy. To him this was sheer impertinence. James believed in the Divine Right of Kings. He thought that his power as King had been granted to him by God and that his wishes had therefore the same force as those of God himself. If he wanted the advice of Parliament he would ask for it. Otherwise the Commons should keep quiet and concentrate on obeying his commands. The Puritan merchants in the Commons could not agree. If they believed that a Catholic royal marriage threatened the Protestant religion, then they thought they had the right – or even the duty – to protest. Thus, when James complained of their conduct and told them to mind their own business, they defied him. To end the argument, James dissolved Parliament. Meanwhile the negotiations for the marriage went on.

The trip to Spain   1623

James's chief minister at this time was a very ambitious young man named George Villiers. He was dashing, handsome and charming, but not very capable. James was very fond of Villiers and had made him Duke of Buckingham and given him unlimited power. Buckingham had a plan which he thought would bring the marriage negotiations to a successful conclusion and he tried to persuade James to agree to it. He proposed that he and Prince Charles, who was at this time twenty-three years old, should go off to Spain in disguise and, after a whirlwind romance, bring the princess back with them. James was ill, but was not easily persuaded. He wept and screamed 'I shall lose Baby Charles', and all his other courtiers advised against the journey. But in the end James wearily gave way and on 7 February 1623 'Jack and Tom Smith' embarked at Dover. After travelling across France the 'dear venturous knights' reached Madrid on 7 March.

War with Spain

To their surprise, they found a very cold welcome awaiting them. The Spanish, far from being swept off their feet, were shocked at this way of going on, and Charles and Buckingham made no progress at all. When they came back, it was without the princess. James was delighted to see them for he had been terrified lest anything should happen to his 'sweet boys', but Buckingham was furious with the Spanish and demanded that England should go to war with Spain at once. James protested but he was almost alone in wanting peace. After all, Spain was England's traditional enemy. At last, James, too ill to care any more, gave way and called Parliament to grant money for the war. The House of Commons were only too pleased to grant supplies. It was a triumph for them. For years they had been trying to make James see that a war with Spain and a Protestant marriage were the best policies. Now at last he had been persuaded. Accordingly, supplies were voted and war was declared. A few months later James died, leaving Buckingham and Charles to carry on the policy they had forced him to adopt.

This English woodcut shows James I greeting Prince Charles on his return from Spain, October 1623.

Dates to remember

1603   James I became King
1604   Hampton Court Conference
1605   Gunpowder Plot
1624   War with Spain
1625   James died

A silver sixpence dating from the end of James I's reign.

Books to read

J. R. Batten, *A Puritan Preacher,* Oxford University Press
W. J. C. Gill, *The Pilgrim Fathers,* Longmans
F. Grice, *Rebels and Fugitives* (Chapter on Guy Fawkes), Batsford
M. C. Borer, *Famous Rogues* (Chapter on Guy Fawkes) Longmans
J. L. Davies (ed.), *The Gunpowder Plot,* Cape (Jackdaw)
B. L. Picard, *The Tower and the Traitors* (Chapter on Walter Raleigh), Batsford

Things to do

1   Here is a letter written by James to Charles and Buckingham while they were in Spain. They had just written telling him that they had failed to persuade the Spaniards to agree to Charles's marriage to their princess. Read it through carefully, and then answer the questions printed below it.

Greenwich June 14.

My Sweet Boys,

Your letter by Cottington hath stricken me dead; I fear it shall much shorten my days, and I am the more perplexed that I know not how to satisfy the people's expectation here. The fleet that stayed for a wind this fortnight must now be stayed, and I know not what reason I shall pretend for the doing of it. But as for my advice and directions that ye crave, in case they will not alter their decree, it is, in a word, to come speedily away, and if ye can get leave, give over all treaty. And this I speak without respect of any security they can offer you, except ye never look to see your old dad again, whom I fear ye shall not see if you see him not before winter. Alas, I now repent me more than ever I suffered you to go away. I care for match, nor nothing, so I may once have you in my arms again. God grant it, God grant it, God grant it, amen, amen, amen. I protest ye shall be as heartily welcome as if ye had done all things ye went for; and God bless you both, my only sweet son, and my only best sweet servant, and let me hear from you quickly, with all speed, as ye love my life; and so God send you a happy and joyful meeting in the arms of your dear dad,

James R.

(a)   What was the people's expectation that James was not going to be able to satisfy?
(b)   What do you think was the purpose of the fleet which would not now have to sail?
(c)   Why did James tell Charles and Buckingham to hurry back?
(d)   What can you learn of James's character from this letter?

my lord out of the loue i beare to some of youer frendz i haue acaer of youer preseruacion therfor i would aduise yowe as yowe tender youer lyf to deuise some erscuse to shift of youer attendance at this parleament for god and man hathe concurred to punishe the wickednes of this tyme and thinke not slightlye of this advertisment but retyere youre self into youre contri wheare yowe maye expect the event in safti for thowghe theare be no apparance of anni stir yet i saye they shall receyue a terrible blowe this parleament and yet they shall not seie who hurts them this councel is not to be contemned becaus it maye do yowe good and can do yowe no harme for the dangere is passed as soon as yowe haue burnt the letter and i hope god will giue yowe the grace to mak good use of it to whose holy proteccion i comend yowe

Nobody knows who wrote this letter. It begins 'my lord out of the love i beare to some of youere frends . . .'

2 Try to copy out the letter sent to Lord Monteagle, which is reproduced above. Remember that the spelling will be different from that used today.

3 Puritans often gave themselves odd names, like 'Praise God' Barebones. See if you can find any more.

4 Find out from the public library if there is a published history of your own town or village, or if there is a county history. Using the local histories which are available, find out which of the important seventeenth-century local families were Catholic and which Puritan.

Family tree, showing James Stuart's claim to the English crown. (He was James VI of Scotland before he became James I of England.)

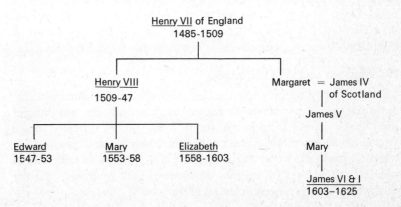

Henry VII of England
1485-1509

Henry VIII
1509-47

Margaret = James IV of Scotland

James V

Edward
1547-53

Mary
1553-58

Elizabeth
1558-1603

Mary

James VI & I
1603-1625

Chapter 2
Charles at peace   1625-42

The situation in 1625

Charles's position was not easy. The House of Commons were pleased
to be at war with Spain, but did not trust the King or Buckingham.
They therefore wanted some control over the conduct of the war. On
the other hand, Charles, like James, believed that he had a God-given
right to do as he pleased without consulting anybody. He was determined to keep the Commons in their place. A quarrel was inevitable.

In fact, Charles left the organization of the war to Buckingham, who
decided on a really spectacular campaign. He wanted to show both the
English and the Spanish that England was a great naval power as she
had been in the age of Drake. He therefore prepared an expedition to
the great Spanish port of Cadiz, which he hoped to capture. Then it
would return to England, bringing huge sums of ransom money, and
covering him and the country with glory.

Cadiz

Everything went wrong. Many of the men were unfit, and the ships
were old and unseaworthy. They were short of food, water, arms and
ammunition. What was worse, the commander, Lord Wimbledon, was
not really up to the task. The ramshackle fleet sailed south and eventually reached Cadiz Bay. There a large Spanish fleet lay at anchor, but
the sailors refused to attack it. When the troops were landed, they
quickly found stores of wine and got so drunk that all that could be
done was to get them back on board as quickly as possible. At his wits'
end, Wimbledon set sail again in the hope of waylaying a Spanish treasure fleet, but he had no success. Meanwhile his men were dying of
thirst and starvation – every day bodies were thrown into the sea. As if
this were not enough, they ran into a great storm and several ships were
sunk. Thus, when the remnants of the expedition reached England,
they were a sorry sight – starving sailors died in the very streets of
Plymouth. Watching them, furious but helpless, stood Sir John Eliot.

Buckingham and the Commons

Eliot was a Puritan, who represented Cornwall in the House of Commons. He was deeply moved by the suffering he had seen and thought
that Buckingham was to blame for it. Many others, ashamed at the
failure of the expedition, agreed with him. Their chance came in 1626
when Charles called Parliament to grant him supplies to carry on the
war. He felt fairly confident that the money would be granted, for the
Commons had always been in favour of the war.

Buckingham must have been
very proud of his legs, otherwise he would never have
had them painted so long in
proportion to the rest of him.

To his amazement Charles found that the Commons would grant nothing. Instead he was met with a torrent of complaints, all directed at Buckingham. 'Our honour is ruined, our ships are sunk, our men perished; not by the sword, not by the enemy, not by chance, but by those we trust.' Thus spoke Sir John Eliot. So far as he was concerned Buckingham was 'the canker in the King's treasure'. 'By him come all our evils, in him we find the causes and on him must be the remedies.' Charles protested, and warned the Commons: 'Parliaments are altogether in my power for their calling, sitting and dissolutions; therefore as I find the fruits of them good or evil, they are to continue or not to be.' Eliot and his friends took no notice, but continued to attack Buckingham. Charles dissolved Parliament.

The second expedition

This was all very well. He had stopped Parliament's mouth, but he still had no money, and he had to get some, for Buckingham was preparing another expedition, this time to France. Desperate, Charles forced merchants and gentry to lend him money. Those who refused were either imprisoned or had soldiers billeted on them. With the funds thus raised, Buckingham fitted out his expedition. It was another failure.

The towns marked on this map are those to which Buckingham sent expeditions between 1625 and 1628.

19

The Petition of Right 1628

This second failure was a terrible blow for Charles to bear, for he had relied on the expedition to win the House of Commons over to his side. Now he would have to meet Parliament and ask them to pay for an expedition which had failed. To make matters worse, Buckingham was already preparing another force to launch against France. This too, had to be paid for. When Parliament met, all Charles's worst fears were realized. Many of the members had spent some time in prison for refusing to lend money to the King, and they were all upset by Buckingham's failures. In the end, however, Charles managed to get some money from them, but only after he had agreed to the Petition of Right, by which he promised not to levy any taxes in future without their consent, not to imprison people without giving a reason, and not to billet soldiers on people in peacetime.

The death of Buckingham

Meanwhile, in Portsmouth all was bustle and confusion, for Buckingham was completing the preparations for his expedition. Even early in the morning he was pestered with crowds of officers, shipwrights and contractors of all sorts, each with his problem for the Duke's decision. As soon as he appeared, there was a rush towards him, everybody trying to get his question in first. But Buckingham answered none of them. He suddenly stopped short in the middle of the crowd, muttered one or two incoherent words, and slumped down. He was caught and supported by one or two of those pressing round him, but he was dead. At first it was thought he had had a fit, but then blood was seen spreading over his clothes, and it was found that he had been stabbed to the heart. Nobody had seen the blow struck, but John Felton, a lieutenant in the navy, was found standing in the Duke's kitchen, and freely admitted that he was the murderer. He said he had done it because he thought the Duke ought to have promoted him to captain, and because so many men in Parliament had said so much against Buckingham.

Felton was hanged, and the expedition was abandoned. When the news of the assassination was brought to London, Charles 'threw himself on his bed, lamenting with much passion and with abundance of tears the loss he had of an excellent servant,' Londoners, on the other hand, lit bonfires in the street, and rang the church bells in glee.

Parliament, which was still sitting, now found their chief enemy gone. Instead of trying to get on good terms with the King, they decided to return to the attack. This was the last straw, and in 1629, Charles dissolved Parliament, determined not to call another if he could avoid it.

Eleven years of personal rule 1629–40

By 1629, then, Charles was dissatisfied with Parliament, and they were angry with him. His actions during the next eleven years, when he ruled without calling Parliament at all, made his opponents, especially the Puritans, even more angry. Not that Charles cared. So far as he was

One of many paintings of Charles I by Van Dyck. The sash over the King's left shoulder is the ribbon of the Order of the Garter. Charles, as usual, has a dignified air.

concerned, they were the best years of his reign. He was happily married, and had a growing family to which he was devoted. He loved good painting, encouraged famous artists to come to England and even knighted two of them, Sir Anthony Van Dyck, the portrait painter, and Sir Peter Paul Rubens, both from the Netherlands. Soon he had built up a fine collection of paintings. Moreover Charles, although small and slow-thinking, was also very dignified and well-mannered, and quickly made his court one of the best conducted in Europe. Here he could feel secure and happy.

Charles I's children, painted in 1637. *Left to right:* Mary (future mother of William III); James, Duke of York (later James II); Charles, Prince of Wales (later Charles II), aged seven; Elizabeth; and Anne, who died as a baby.

Strafford and Laud

To replace Buckingham, Charles now had faithful and efficient ministers, the most famous of whom were Thomas Wentworth, Earl of Strafford, and William Laud, Archbishop of Canterbury. Strafford was a hard, stern man who spent much of his time in Ireland, which he ruled with a rod of iron. He advised the King on how to govern England without a Parliament, and Charles found that by reviving old laws and taxes which had been long forgotten, and by using the Court of Star Chamber set up by the Tudors to enforce them, he could manage to get enough money to keep going. The merchants and landowners who had to pay such taxes did not like them, and sometimes tried to prove that they were illegal by taking cases to court, but the judges always said that they had to pay. This made them very angry and they hated and feared

Strafford but could do nothing to get rid of him so long as Charles did not call a Parliament.

Charles's other minister, Archbishop Laud, was just as unpopular, but for quite different reasons. Laud believed that the more ceremony there was in a church service, and the more beautiful the church, the greater would be the religious devotion of the congregation. This was exactly the opposite to what the Puritans believed. They thought that ceremony and ornament distracted the worshipper from his prayers and were therefore harmful. Below, you will see two pictures. One of these is a church as Laud wanted it, and the other as the Puritans liked it. From them you will see in how many ways they differed.

When Laud became Archbishop, there were many Church of England clergy who agreed with the Puritans, and had done away with much of the pomp and ceremony of the Church. Laud had no patience with them. 'Tis superstition nowadays', he grumbled, 'for any man to come with more reverence into a church than a tinker and his bitch come into an ale house.' All this had to stop. The Church must be treated with respect, and the services made as beautiful as possible, with robes for the priest, ceremonial and music. Those clergy who refused to obey Laud were liable to be punished by the Court of High Commission which was controlled by the bishops. As a result many clergy left the Church and the Puritans hated Laud, for they feared that he really wanted to bring back Catholicism.

Two engravings. *Left:* how Laud wished a church to be. *Right:* how the Puritans liked it.

Seventeenth-century punishments. A man *(left)* being whipped at the cart's tail; another *(centre)* stands in the pillory. On the right are the gallows at Tyburn. This picture is English. Notice how poor its quality is compared with the Dutch engravings.

Puritan pamphlets

This meant that to Puritans Laud was everything that was evil, and that his brother bishops were no better. Nor were the Puritans slow to say what they thought. 'Praise God' Barebones could be heard thundering against the bishops at his religious meetings on Sundays, and so could many others like him. Some were not content to preach, but also printed pamphlets attacking Laud and his policies. Some of them were very violent. John Bastwick, a doctor, wrote that bishops were 'the most wicked, profane and unconscionable men that live upon the earth, and inferior to the Pope in no impiety'. The clergy were 'a generation of vipers, of proud ungrateful idle, wicked and illiterate asses', and cathedrals were 'so many dens of thieves and cages of filthiness and idolatry'. Another writer, Alexander Leighton, had called the bishops 'bloody beasts' and 'knobs and wens of bunchy popish flesh'. In 1637 these two, together with William Prynne, a lawyer, who hated theatres and bishops about equally, were tried by the Court of Star Chamber, and sentenced to be whipped, put in the pillory, have their ears cut off, pay huge fines and be imprisoned for life. Charles was determined to show his subjects that he supported Laud but, when the Puritans' ears were cut off in the pillory, the vast crowd which watched booed and jeered not at the prisoners, but at the executioner, and it turned into a kind of triumph for the three pamphleteers.

Charles and Scotland

But however discontented people in England might be, they could do nothing unless the King called Parliament, and he had no intention of doing this. Indeed, he felt so secure that he decided to try to reform the Church in Scotland in the same way that Laud had reformed the Church of England. The Scots, however, were still far more Puritan than the English, and when Charles tried to introduce a new prayer book into Scotland, it was greeted with riots and rebellions on such a scale that

24

A Scottish clergyman tries to read a service from Laud's new prayer book. Stools were quite a usual form of seating in Scottish churches.

even the Scots were surprised. Charles was determined to get his way, and sent an army into Scotland, but found the Scottish army too good for him. He therefore called Parliament, but they seemed uncooperative and so were soon sent packing. The Scots at once overran Northumberland and Durham, and refused to move until Charles had promised to respect their religion and paid them an enormous sum of money in compensation. Charles had no money left, and so called another Parliament, hoping that at this time of peril everybody would rally round against the Scots.

The Long Parliament   1640–42

He was disappointed. Parliament would do nothing to help him. The Puritan merchants in the Commons felt more sympathy with the Scots than they did with Charles. They, like the Scots, wished to be rid of Laud and his prayer book. What was more, they were furious that so many years had passed without Parliament meeting. They had always wanted a greater say in the government of the country. Instead of that

Some of Charles's troops, sent to fight the Scots, destroyed the altar rails and took away the ornaments in an English church. Clearly they liked Laud as little as did the Scots.

The Court of High Commission in session. All the members are bishops, in all their finery.

they had been completely ignored. They were determined it must not happen again.

'We must', said John Pym, the leader of the opposition to the King in the House of Commons, 'be of another temper than we were the last Parliament; we must not only sweep the house clean below, but pull down all the cobwebs which hang in the top and corners, that they may not breed dust and so make a foul house hereafter.'

The end of Strafford

First, the Commons turned on Charles's ministers, imprisoning both Strafford and Laud. The Archbishop was left in prison, but their hatred and fear of Strafford was such that they decided to bring him to trial before the House of Lords on a charge of treason. Their charge was based on the accusation that Strafford had written to the King advising him to bring over an army of Irish Catholics to keep England in order. Strafford had, in fact, sent a letter to the King from Ireland mentioning that there was an army available there but he had intended that the King should use it in Scotland, not England. Thus the Commons, who were seething with terror and hatred at the very thought of Irish Catholics, really made a mistake in accusing Strafford of treason, for it was going to be impossible to prove the charge.

It was no wonder that Strafford smiled when he heard the charge read, or that the Lords showed quite clearly that they were going to find him 'not guilty'. The Commons realized their mistake, dropped the case, and instead brought in a special act of Parliament, which simply said that Strafford was guilty of high treason and must be executed. The Commons passed this easily, and a great mob of Londoners, shouting for 'Death to Black Tom Tyrant', so terrified the members of the Lords that they passed it too. It was now up to the King. He had promised Strafford that he would not be harmed, but now, with the shouts of the mob ringing in his ears, he was brought a letter from the Tower, in which

Strafford released him from this promise. 'To a willing man', he wrote, 'there is no injury done – to you I can give the life of the world with all cheerfulness imaginable.' After a week-end's hesitation, Charles signed the act, and Strafford was executed on Tower Hill in front of a vast crowd. As the executioner held up his head for the crowd to see, horsemen galloped off through the countryside triumphantly shouting, 'His head is off, his head is off', and bonfires were kindled in the streets.

The arrest of the five members

With Strafford out of the way, Pym and his friends carried on with their work of 'sweeping the house clean'. They passed acts making it impossible for the King to get money without Parliament's consent. Another act abolished the Courts of Star Chamber and High Commission, which had been so useful to Charles in the past few years. Then they made another law saying that Parliament had to be called every three years,

The execution of Strafford, 1641. 100,000 people are said to have been there. Many of them can have seen nothing, and the galleries on which they were standing seem far from safe.

A Docto
te of
B the sh
C the E
D. his ki

and finally, one to say that they could not be dissolved without their own consent. Only after the King had given his consent to all these would they grant the money to pay the Scots and get them to leave the country. Many members now thought that they had gone far enough, but a majority of them wanted next to begin work on the Church, in order to make it more Puritan. Charles would never allow them to do this, and decided to show them who was master by arresting five of their leaders on a charge of treason. He set out for Parliament with a number of soldiers, and entered the House of Commons, but was too late. They had heard he was on the way, and the five members had been sent off into hiding.

The outbreak of the Civil War   1642

Charles had now really upset the Commons. They resented his forcing his way into the House to arrest five of their number, and it made them fear that if ever he could get the upper hand again he might make them suffer. They therefore decided to take control of the army, which was bound to be enlarged to deal with a rebellion which had just broken out in Ireland. But Charles would have none of it. When it was pointed out that he might only have to give up control of the army for a short time, he answered, 'By God! not for an hour! You have asked that of me in this was never asked of a king, and with which I will not trust my wife and children.' Shortly after this he left London, and Parliament passed an act taking over the army from the King, saying it did not need his consent. Charles's answer was to call on all his subjects to rally round and help him to put the Commons in their place.

The country divides

Thus the great Civil War began. It was a conflict which sometimes divided families and ended old friendships. As you might expect, the Puritans tended to support Parliament. Charles had shown by his sup-

This musketeer has just fired. In his left hand is a smouldering match; pouches of powder hang from a belt over his shoulder.

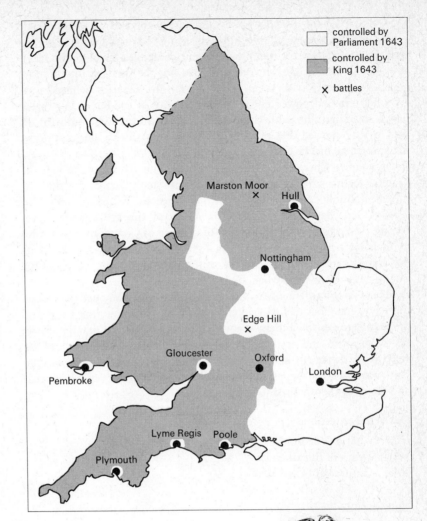

controlled by
Parliament 1643

controlled by
King 1643

× battles

Marston Moor
×
Hull

Nottingham

Edge Hill
×

Gloucester
Oxford
London

Pembroke

Lyme Regis
Poole

Plymouth

This map shows the area
controlled by Parliament in
1643, and the names of the
important battles fought in
the early years of the war.

A pikeman, the end of his pike
firmly wedged against his
left foot. He steadies the
weapon with his right hand,
leaving his left hand free to
draw his sword.

port of Laud that his policy was completely opposed to theirs. They were joined by the merchants and industrialists, which meant that Parliament could draw on their wealth, and controlled most of the large towns. These men felt that the King had not the smallest intention of sharing his power with them. They were right. Charles believed that God had granted power not to the people, but to the King. 'A subject and a sovereign', he said, 'are clean different things.' The outbreak of war in 1642 showed that this attitude was no answer to the great problems which he had faced.

Of course, Charles had supporters too. The Church of England, grateful for his support against the Puritans, stood firm by his side. So did the Catholics, who feared what might become of them if men like 'Praise God' Barebones got control. Many of the great landowners, feeling their position threatened by the House of Commons, also threw in their lot with Charles. This was a great advantage to him, for they had huge fortunes, which they put at the King's disposal. This enabled him to put an army in the field by the autumn of 1642.

Meanwhile, Parliament too had been recruiting. They had control of the navy, for Charles had seldom paid the sailors. Now, the wealth of the merchants enabled them to equip an army, which was mainly drawn from the south and east. Charles, on the other hand, got most of his support in the north and west where there were fewer towns and the landowners were strongest. The sides thus seemed to be evenly balanced, and the struggle promised to be a long one.

Dates to remember

1625   Charles I became king
1628   Death of Buckingham
1642   Outbreak of Civil War

Things to do

1   Here is a letter written to Strafford by Charles I. Read it through carefully and then answer the questions on page 31.

A Charles I silver shilling, struck in the Royal Mint at the Tower of London.

Whitehall
April 23, 1641.

Strafford,

The misfortune that is fallen upon you by the strange mistaking and conjuncture of these times, being such that I must lay by the thought of employing you hereafter in my affairs; yet I cannot satisfy myself in honour and conscience without assuring you (now in the midst of your troubles), that upon the word of a King you shall not suffer in life, honour, or fortune. This is but justice, and therefore a very mean reward from a master to so faithful and able a servant as you have showed yourself to be; yet it is as much as I conceive the present times will permit, though none shall hinder me from being

Your constant, faithful friend,
Charles R.

(a) Where was Strafford when this letter was written?

(b) Why did the King think it necessary to promise that Strafford should not suffer 'in life, honour, or fortune'?

(c) What does this letter reveal of Charles's character? Remember what happened to Strafford.

2 Try to see pictures of Strafford, Pym and Laud. You will find them in many books.

3 Try to find out something more about the Courts of High Commission and Star Chamber.

4 One of the taxes which Charles levied between 1629 and 1640 was called 'Ship Money'. Try to find out something about it, and about John Hampden, who refused to pay it.

Things to discuss

Could Charles I have done anything which would have prevented the Civil War from breaking out?

Books to read

F. Grice, *Rebels and Fugitives* (Chapter on John Hampden), Batsford

K. Moore, *Richard Baxter – Toleration and Tyranny*, Longmans

P. Rush, *Strange Stuarts* (Chapter on John Felton), Hutchinson

Chapter 3
The Civil War and the Commonwealth

Rupert's cavalry

In 1645, the war had been going on for three years, and the Scots had come in on the side of Parliament. In the early years of the war, the King had had the better of it. This was because he had the better army. In particular, his cavalry, commanded by his nephew Prince Rupert, was famous. It consisted of gentry, who had always been used to hunting, and were thus skilled and fearless horsemen. Prince Rupert had, moreover, served in Europe during the Thirty Years War and had brought back with him new ideas about cavalry fighting. Until the middle of the seventeenth century it was the custom for the cavalry to charge up to the enemy, stop, fire their pistols, and then rush in with their swords. Rupert's men charged pell-mell at their enemies, crashed into them at full gallop, and did not stop until they had driven them from the field. Again and again the Royalist cavalry had swept their opponents aside, and more than one battle might have been won outright if only Rupert had been able to gather his cavalry together quickly after such a charge and bring them back to the battlefield to help the royal infantry. But by the time the enthusiastic horsemen drew rein, it was either too late, or else the horses were so blown that they could not charge again that day.

Cavaliers and Roundheads.

The coming of the Ironsides

Some of the leaders of the Parliamentary army had seen that, if they were to win the war, then they would have to have cavalry as good as Rupert's. Colonel Cromwell, for instance, realized in 1643 that it was no good expecting an ordinary working man, whose heart was not really in the fight, to stand up against these self-confident gentry. What was needed was men who knew what they were fighting for, and were prepared to give up everything, including their lives, for it. Cromwell set about finding such men. He went recruiting round the East Midlands and soon had the makings of a fine fighting force. His men were steady, sober yeomen and townsmen, respectable, Puritan, God-fearing men. They were men who wanted to fight against the King because they thought his policies were wicked; who were, like Cromwell himself, convinced they were fighting on God's side. Certain that they had God's blessing, this army did not, like some, drink rum or gin to give them courage. Instead they heard sermons and sang hymns. In battle their cry was 'God our strength'. They were trained to charge as Rupert's

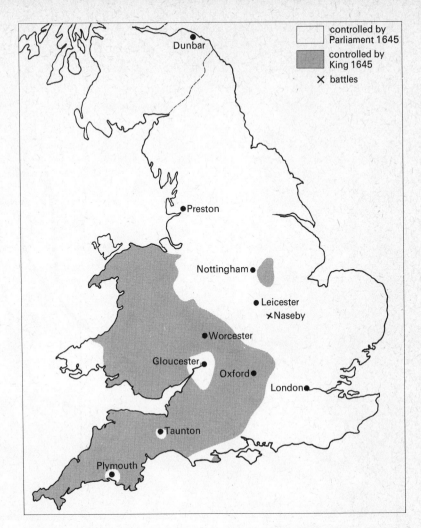

Parliament, with the help of
the Scots, had gained control
of the north of England by
1645.

men did, and proved so steady when attacked that Rupert himself called
them 'Ironsides'. The name stuck.

The New Model Army

The first battle in which the Ironsides proved themselves was the Battle
of Marston Moor in 1644 where Rupert was defeated and the north of
England was lost to the King. They were so impressive that Parliament
decided to set up a whole 'New Model Army', organized in the same way.
They were to be paid regularly, properly equipped, and very strictly
disciplined. Their commander was Sir Thomas Fairfax – a fine soldier.
Second in command was General Cromwell. Soon, from volunteers and
conscripts, Parliament had an army of 20,000 men, ready to fight anywhere in England. There were many important battles in the Civil War,
but to give you an idea of how battles were fought in those days, here is
an account of one of them, the Battle of Naseby.

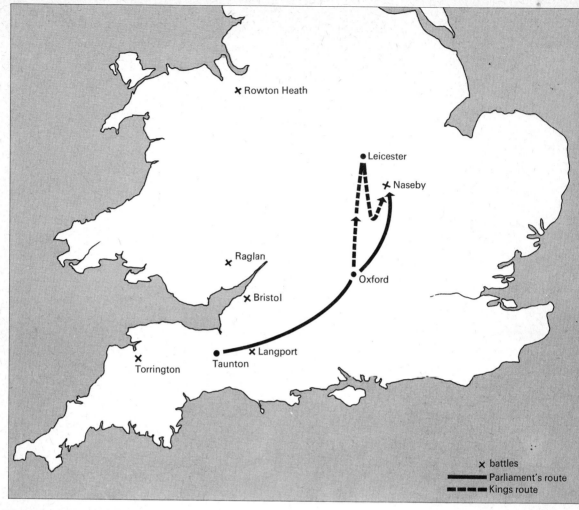

Legend:
✗ battles
▬▬▬ Parliament's route
▬ ▬ ▬ Kings route

The two sides at Naseby 1645

In 1645 the New Model Army was sent to attack the King's head-quarters at Oxford. To draw them off, the King captured Leicester and laid it waste. Fairfax at once set off after Charles and eventually caught up with him at Naseby, near Market Harborough. Here, on top of a ridge, Charles had drawn up his army, facing south. Three-quarters of a mile in front of him was another ridge and Fairfax drew up his forces along this, covering a front of just over a mile. In the centre, Fairfax put his pikemen, most of them with no armour. They were armed with swords and with pikes up to eighteen feet long. On each side of them were the musketeers, armed with muzzle-loading muskets, which were fired by igniting the powder with a smouldering piece of string called a match. These weapons were useless if it was raining and took about three minutes to reload. Their range was about 400 yards. Usually the musketeers were drawn up in six ranks, and, when the first rank had

Movements of the King and Fairfax before the Battle of Naseby. The other battles marked were fought during 1645 and 1646. Naseby was not the only one, simply the most important.

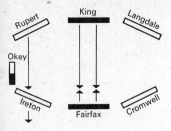

1 The armies are drawn up and the King's army charges.

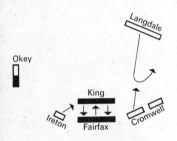

2 Langdale's charge is repulsed by Cromwell. Rupert has charged from the field.

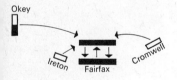

3 The King's infantry are surrounded.

Pages 36–37 This plan of the two armies drawn up before the Battle of Naseby is not to scale. The two armies were nearly a mile apart, and the Parliamentary army covered a front nearly twice as long as did that of the King. Nor did Charles I lead his troops. He remained behind with the reserve.

fired, they went to the rear to reload. Then the second rank fired and went on to the back, and so on. In this way a more or less continuous fire could be kept up at the rate of a volley every half-minute as long as the ammunition lasted. Each man was paid eightpence a day, a labourer's wage. Many of them were conscripted.

To complete the line, Fairfax put cavalry on each side, those on the left under the command of General Ireton, those on the right under Cromwell himself. These cavalrymen, paid two shillings a day, were armed with a sword and a pair of pistols each. For protection they wore back and breast plates and helmets. Most of them were volunteers. Next, far over to the left, and at right-angles to the main line, Fairfax drew up a troop of dragoons under Colonel Okey. Dragoons were neither infantry nor cavalry. They had horses to get from place to place, but usually fought on foot. They wore no armour, and carried swords and short muskets. They were paid one and sixpence a day, and were used to guard roads and hedges. Last of all, a few guns, firing solid iron shot, were drawn up into the gaps between the regiments, but they played little part in the battle. By 10 a.m. all was ready.

The battle begins

Meanwhile, the King had been drawing up his army in the same sort of pattern, with the infantry in the middle and cavalry on each flank. For a few minutes the two armies faced each other. Then, from the King's army came a rolling of drums and shouting of orders, and the Royalist pikemen and musketeers began to advance. Down the hill they came, and began to climb the gentle slope to where the Parliamentary infantry were advancing to meet them. As the two lines of shouting, struggling men came to grips, Prince Rupert ordered his cavalry on the right to charge. They thundered down the hill, past Colonel Okey and his dragoons, up past the struggling infantry, now fighting hand to hand, and crashed into Ireton's cavalry. For a time Ireton's men held them, but they were not such good swordsmen as the Royalists, and first in ones and twos, and then in great numbers, they began to ride away. Soon they were in full flight, leaving their commander with only a few horsemen on the flank they had been protecting. Rupert and his men rode after the fleeing men, pursuing them right through Naseby village, and attacking the Parliamentary supply train which they found there. It was over an hour before Rupert could bring his tired but triumphant men back to the battlefield.

The battle is won

In the meantime, the result of the battle was decided. The King's infantry in the centre fought with such determination that the Parliamentary infantry were only saved by a desperate charge by Ireton and his few remaining horsemen, which resulted in Ireton's capture. Thus, when Sir Marmaduke Langdale launched his cavalry from the King's left to help the Royalist infantry, it seemed as if the New Model Army

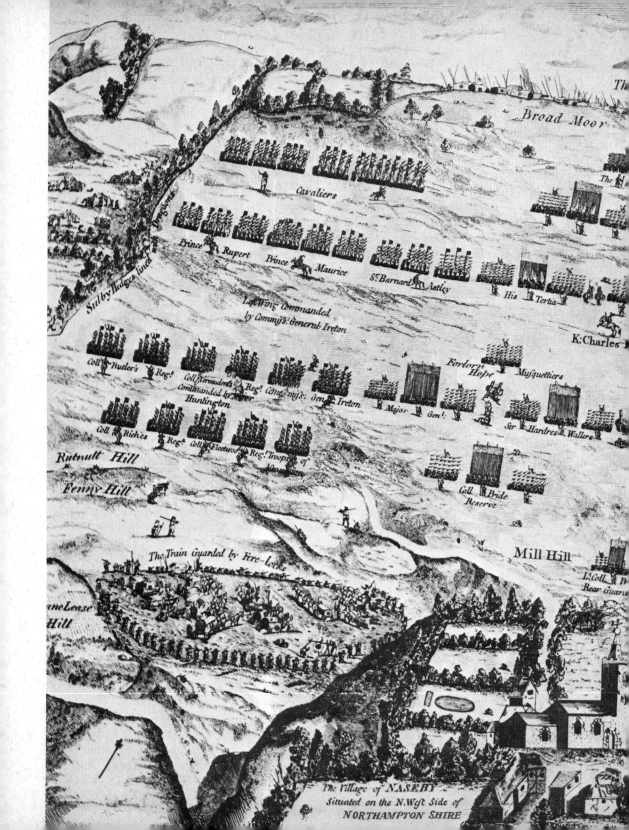

Broad Moor

The

Cavaliers

The

Prince Rupert Prince Maurice Sr Barnard Astley His Tertia

Silbby Hedges lined with Dragounes

K: Charles

Left Wing Commanded
by Commiss.^s Generall Ireton

Coll Butler's Reg.^t Coll Varmudens Reg.^t Commiss.^s Genl Ireton Major Genl Forlorn Hope Musquettiers
Commanded by Major Huntington

Sir Hardres Wallers

Coll Riches Reg.^t Coll Fleetwoods Reg.^t Troopes of

Rutnutt Hill

Fenny Hill

Coll Pride Reserve

Mill Hill

The Train Guarded by Fire-locks

L. Coll B
Rear Guard

aneLease
Hill

The Village of NASEBY
Situated on the N.West Side of
NORTHAMPTON SHIRE

might be defeated. But it was not to be. Cromwell watched Sir Marmaduke's advance, and, as the Royalist cavalry began to climb the hill
towards his lines, he launched half his cavalry in a thunderbolt charge.
They were irresistible. Langdale's men were swept from the field. Cromwell then sent the other half of his force crashing into the flank of the
Royalist infantry.

As if this were not enough, Colonel Okey, seeing his chance, ordered
his dragoons to mount their horses and charge – a thing they very
rarely did. Within a few minutes Okey's men hit the Royalists on the
other flank. The King's men fought bravely, but hopelessly. They were
outnumbered, and hemmed in on three sides. Only reinforcements
could save them, and Charles prepared to lead his last reserves down the
slope to their help. He was stopped by Lord Carnwath, who seized the
bridle of his horse, shouting 'Will you go upon your death?' Charles
might still have gone, but his troops took matters into their own hands
by riding from the field. Meanwhile Rupert and his cavalry had
returned, but their horses were in no condition to charge again. The
battle was lost. Charles rode back to Leicester, leaving his infantry to
die where they stood. In the end more than four thousand of them
were either killed or captured.

Cromwell's report

As for the Parliamentarians, they wiped out those Royalists left on the
battlefield, and then set off in pursuit. They failed to catch the King,
but they knew that they had won a great victory. That same night
Cromwell wrote to the Speaker of the House of Commons about the
battle. 'This day', he said,

An archer. Archers still fought
in the Civil War.

we marched towards him. He drew out to meet us. Both armies engaged.
We, after three hours' fight, very doubtful, at last routed his army, killed and
took about five thousand, very many officers, but of what quality we yet know
not. We took also about two hundred carriages, all he had, and all his guns,
being twelve in number, whereof two were demi-cannon, two demi-culverins
and (I think) the rest sacers. We pursued the enemy from three miles short of
Harborough to nine beyond, even to the sight of Leicester, whither the King
fled. Sir, this is none other but the hand of God, and to Him alone belongs
the glory.

The army take charge

Naseby was the last major battle of the Civil War and in 1646 old
General Astley, commanding the last Royalist force left fighting, handed
over his sword to Parliamentary officers. 'You have done your work',
he said as he wearily seated himself on a drum, 'and may now go play,
unless you fall out among yourselves.' It was, in fact, not long before the
victorious Parliamentarians were quarrelling with each other just as
violently as they had with the Royalists. On the one hand the House of
Commons and the Scots felt that Charles had been taught a lesson, and
were willing to let him continue as King, provided that he was willing

to give up some of his power. The army, on the other hand, wanted to punish him for his crimes.

For a time, the Commons had their way, and tried to make a treaty with the King. In 1647, they even felt strong enough to disband the army. But many in the army did not think they were being treated fairly, and thought it was time they took a hand. A party of them rode to Holmby, where the King was negotiating with Parliamentary commissioners, and told him to come away. When Charles heard this, he asked one of them by what authority he was acting, and demanded to see his commission. In answer, the soldier pointed through the window to the troops waiting outside. The King smiled. 'It is as fair a commission,' he said, 'and as well written as I have seen a commission in my life.' The troopers took him away.

Charles and the Scots

For a year Charles bargained with the army and the Commons. The war had taught him nothing. So far as he was concerned, his opponents were mere rebels, who deserved a traitor's death. In the long run, he was not prepared to give up any of the power which God had granted him. In the meantime, he was forced to play for time.

Finally, in 1648, his chance came. He was able to make a bargain with the Scots behind Parliament's back, and arrange for a Scottish army to invade England. In 1648 it came south and was defeated at Preston. Cromwell and his generals were furious. The King had betrayed them and had plunged the country into war once more. It was impossible to make treaties with such a man, for you could not trust him to keep his word. He deserved to be tried and punished for his wickedness. Many members of Parliament did not agree. In spite of all they still wanted to come to terms with Charles. The army officers had no time for such faint-heartedness and sent Colonel Pride down to the House of Commons to turn out all those who were not in favour of punishing the King. He did his job well, and the eighty members who were left set up a court to try Charles. The judges who were chosen were convinced of the King's guilt from the start. They merely wanted to show the country how great a criminal he was before they executed him.

The King's trial and execution

It did not turn out as they expected. First, some of the judges refused to have anything to do with the trial. For instance Fairfax retired to his estates in Yorkshire rather than become involved. This was a bad start, but, more important, the whole trial was dominated by the King himself! This small, dignified man, dressed from head to foot in black, usually so slow of thought and speech, never put a foot wrong. He simply pointed out that the court set up to try him was completely illegal, and refused to put his case to it. Twice, after long arguments, they ordered him to be taken away, with nothing achieved. The third day, when ordered to answer the charge, he replied as follows:

Sir Thomas Fairfax in 1647.

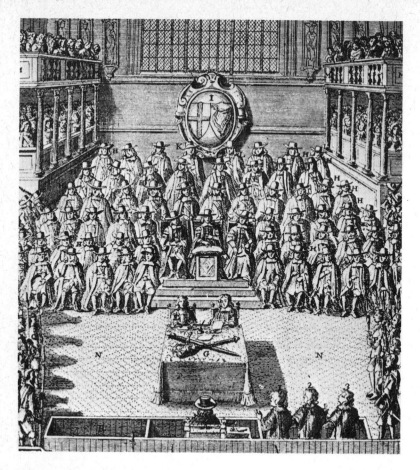

Left: the King's trial, held in Westminster Hall. Charles sits *(centre)*, his back to us, facing his judges. John Bradshaw, president of the court, is immediately opposite him.

Right: this Dutch engraving shows Charles's execution. The place, in Whitehall, was carefully chosen. It was big enough to accommodate a fair sized crowd, but small cnough to be cleared quickly. The Banqueting Hall still stands. The rest of Whitehall Palace was burned down in 1689.

For me to acknowledge a new court, that I never heard of before, I that am your King, that should be an example to all the people of England, indeed I do not know how to do it. I do acknowledge to God that I owe to Him and to my people to defend as much as in me lies the ancient laws of the kingdom: therefore until that I may know that this is not against the fundamental laws of the kingdom, by your favour I can put in no particular charge.

The judges were unable to shake the King's determination. They were in a difficult position. They had brought him to trial to show everybody how he had made war on the liberty of the people, and now he was claiming to be defending the people's liberty against them! The thing was absurd.

Finally, they decided to get the whole business over as quickly as possible. The next time the King was brought before the court, he was pronounced guilty and sentenced to death by beheading. His death warrant was signed by fifty-nine judges. Two days later, on 30 January 1649, Charles was taken to a scaffold specially built outside his palace of Whitehall and there, at 2 p.m., his head was chopped off. 'The blow I saw given', wrote one onlooker, 'and can truly say with a sad heart.

An eighteenth-century engraving of Charles I's death warrant. The original is not so clear. Cromwell's signature is on the left.

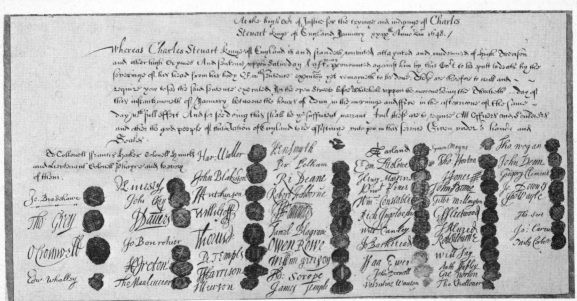

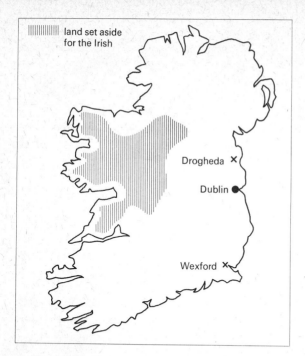

land set aside for the Irish

Drogheda ×

Dublin ●

Wexford ×

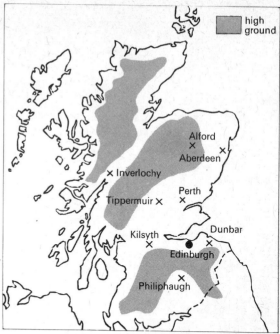

high ground

Alford ×
Aberdeen ×
× Inverlochy
Perth ×
Tippermuir ×
Dunbar
Kilsyth × × ×
Edinburgh ●
Philiphaugh ×

At the instant, whereof I remember well, there was such a groan by the thousands there present as I never heard before, and desire I may never again.' England was a republic.

Cromwell takes charge

The execution of the King left the army in control. Since Fairfax had retired, the commander-in-chief was now Oliver Cromwell. For a year or two his army was busy. First, there was a rebellion in Ireland to be crushed. Cromwell did this by massacring the garrisons of all towns which refused to surrender, with the result that others quickly opened their gates. Once the fighting was over, he took land from the Catholics and gave it to Protestants, so that England would, in future, be sure to have some friends in Ireland. Then there was Scotland. The Scots were furious with the English for having executed Charles, who was, after all, King of Scotland as well as King of England. They therefore crowned his son, Charles II. To settle this, Cromwell invaded Scotland in 1650, and defeated one Scottish army at Dunbar, but the next year another, commanded by Charles himself, invaded England. Cromwell allowed it to get as far south as Worcester before he attacked, and then he routed it completely. Many Scottish nobles were captured, but young Charles escaped to France, after many exciting adventures.

Ideas of government

Meanwhile in England all was not well. Now that the King had gone, the House of Lords was abolished and the country was being governed

These maps show the battles fought in Ireland and Scotland. The area shaded on the map of Ireland is that which Cromwell set aside for the native Irish. With the exception of Dunbar, the battles in Scotland were fought on the King's behalf by the Marquis of Montrose, 1645.

by a few Puritans in the House of Commons who were only there because they were friends of the army. This was not a good system, and people began to try to think of one to replace it. The Royalists wanted simply to bring in Charles II and make everything as it had been before, with the House of Lords, and the Church ruled by bishops. But, although there were many Royalists, they had no power. Many moderate people agreed that it would be a good thing to bring back the monarchy, but did not want to see bishops in charge of the Church. They had no power either. Others, like John Lilburne, wanted to try something completely new. He wanted all men to have a vote to elect members of a House of Commons, which would then rule the country. Some even wanted to abolish all private property, or to hand over the government to ministers of religion.

Now Cromwell really liked none of these ideas. All that he wanted was a fair system which would keep the peace and allow all godly and sincere people to worship as their consciences told them they ought. The ideas of men like Lilburne frightened him. He thought they would lead to chaos, and believed that such men had to be broken, or they would break the State. Accordingly, Lilburne was imprisoned and his beliefs were suppressed. This, of course, made Cromwell very unpopular with some of Lilburne's friends. They began to

A medal struck to commemorate the battle of Dunbar. One side shows Cromwell's bust, with his army's battle cry; the other the House of Commons in session, with far more members present than ever attended between 1648 and 1653.

wonder which side the Commander-in-Chief really supported. Could he be trusted? 'He will lay his hand on his breast,' wrote one, 'elevate his eyes, and call God to record. He will weep, howl and repent even while he doth smite you under the fifth rib.'

Cromwell dismisses Parliament

During all this discussion, the remnant of the House of Commons was carrying on. But they did not seem to be doing any good. Many of them worked hard to increase their own wealth and power, but when they were asked to do anything to make the government of the country more efficient, they were very slow. At last Cromwell and the other army officers lost patience with them. They had not fought and defeated the King simply to benefit these few men. 'These men will never leave till the army pull them out by the ears,' said Cromwell, and one day in

Cromwell turns out the Commons in 1653. The owl *(foreground)* is meant to represent the short-sighted stupidity of the members. Once again, the print is Dutch.

1653, he went down to the Commons with a file of musketeers and turned out all the members with the words: 'I will put an end to your prating, you are no Parliament – I say you are no Parliament.' As the last member hurried out, hustled by the soldiers, the door was locked behind him. The next day someone had chalked on it: 'This House To Let, Unfurnished.'

Now that Parliament, like the King, had gone, Cromwell was left with all the power in his hands. For the next five years, until his death in 1658, he ruled the country, wielding more power than Charles I had ever done. To be fair, he tried hard to set up some sort of Parliament, but he could never get on with them and was always forced in the end to dissolve them. Finally, he was king in all but name, and had nominated his son Richard to succeed him as Lord Protector on his death.

A Puritan family at table. The master of the house keeps his hat on, while the children stand throughout the meal.

Life in Cromwell's England

The years between 1649 and 1660 were strange ones for Englishmen. After all, there was no king, no proper Parliament, and no Church of England. 'Praise God' Barebones and his friends had things their way for once, and they introduced changes which altered many aspects of English life. To begin with, many of the Englishman's traditional amusements were banned. Bull-baiting was forbidden, the cockpits were closed, and the bear-pits empty. Theatres were destroyed, and seven actors who tried to put on a play in Newcastle in 1655 were whipped in the Market Place. Even the maypoles were pulled down, and all religious festivals were abolished, so that at Christmas soldiers went around the streets of London from house to house, pulling meat

45

from the ovens. This was also liable to happen on the last Wednesday of each month which was a fast day. On such days, wrote one Londoner, 'not one of us, young or old, ate so much as a morsel of bread for twenty-four hours together.' If a man were annoyed at the restrictions, he had to be careful not to speak too strongly, for swearing was punishable by a fine of three and fourpence, or three hours in the stocks. One unfortunate man was even fined for saying 'As God is my witness', and another for exclaiming 'Upon my Life'.

The Sabbath

This was good enough for weekdays, but on Sundays the rules were stricter still. 'Praise God' Barebones and his fellow-Puritans had always

The title page of a pamphlet published in 1653. It complains of heavy taxation and the abolition of Christmas. The woodcut shows Father Christmas being driven away from the town by the figure on the left, only to be welcomed by the happy countryman on the right.

'Nick Froth the Tapster and Rulerost the Cook' complain about the Puritan restrictions which forbade the sale of strong meat and drink on Sunday.

believed that Sunday belonged to God, and they now passed laws to make sure that everybody devoted their time on that day to religion and to nothing else. All games and recreations of any sort were banned. It was even illegal to go for a walk, unless it was to attend a religious service in your own parish! Nor could you get on with the housework, for this was against the law, and one poor servant girl was fined ten shillings for doing so, and another was put into the stocks for mending a dress on Sunday. Of course, these laws were difficult to enforce, but there were always informers about who would tell the authorities if they had seen you doing something illegal, and would then get part of the fine as their reward. To control what went on inside the home, officials were allowed to search houses just to make sure that all was well.

The achievements of the Commonwealth

Puritanism had, of course, a positive side as well, which showed itself in a variety of ways. Cromwell's government tried to reform the law, so that justice would be cheap and speedy. They were only partly successful, but it was better than nothing. The faith of some Puritans found expression in great poetry. Cromwell encouraged such poets, making the greatest of them, John Milton, his Latin secretary. Education was reformed. New schools were founded, and an attempt was made to set up a new University at Durham. At the same time, the Commons went to great lengths to protect and encourage England's trade. Although Cromwell did not approve, they passed an act declaring that all goods brought to Britain had to be carried in British ships, or those of the producing country. This led to trouble with the Dutch, who had made a good living carrying goods to and from England. This did not greatly worry the English. As we shall see in Chapter 7, England was quite capable of taking care of herself in a European war.

Religion under the Commonwealth

Cromwell's rule allowed a great degree of religious freedom. The Protector himself was in favour of allowing everyone to worship as he pleased – he even allowed the Jews freedom of worship for the first time since 1290. His views were, however, too revolutionary for his advisers, and in the end Catholicism and the *Book of Common Prayer* were banned. Apart from these, any form of worship was allowed. The result was a sudden growth in the number of religious sects. A foreigner counted seventy-four chapels in Fleet Street alone. In many churches a decent sober service was held, only with a sermon sometimes taking as long as two or three hours. The congregation would sit with their hats on, some of them taking notes as they listened. Sometimes the sermon would mention some current problem. On other occasions they might simply expound some verses from the Bible. In either case, they were liable to be interrupted by shouts and heckling from Quakers, who used to go from church to church to try to stop any service they did not like, which made them very unpopular with the other sects.

The Quakers

Quaker services themselves were liable to be very odd. 'At their meetings,' wrote one reporter, 'after long silence, sometimes one, and sometimes more (as at one time five together) fall into a great and dreadful shaking and trembling of their whole bodies and all their joints, with such risings and swellings, in their bellies and bowels, together with such screechings, yellings, howlings and roarings, which

Even the educated believed in witches. Many innocent old women were tortured to death or were 'dipped' in the river as punishment.

A meeting of Quakers in 1699. Before the meeting begins, the chairman makes sure that the doors are locked and that no outsiders are present.

A French engraving of a Quaker service with a woman preaching. This astonished people in the seventeenth century. The smartly dressed group *(foreground)* are visitors.

doth not only amaze and affright the spectators, but also cause the dogs to bark.' When they had worked themselves into a frenzy, they preached, believing that their words were directly inspired by God. These Quakers were often persecuted, because they had no respect for any ranks, titles, or even governments. They believed that every human being could get directly in touch with God, and that therefore no one man was any more important than any other. Their leader, George Fox, was a great preacher and was able to recruit many followers, one of whom, William Penn, horrified the King's court after the Restoration by standing with his hat on in the presence of Charles II. In spite of years of persecution and imprisonment, the Quakers survived, and, as the Society of Friends, are still with us, accepted and respected members of the community.

Minor sects

Other sects did not last so long. For instance, there were the Aposticals, who believed that every word in the Bible must be literally obeyed. Some of them therefore climbed on to the tops of houses to preach, while others deserted their wives and children and wandered penniless

49

One Evins a Welch man was lately comited to New gate for saying hee was Christ

Iesuit — *Arminian* — *Arian* — *Adamite* — *Libertin*

Heers one blasphemously That sed was christ did say Such spirits were foretold To rise ith latter daye

Ante scripturian — *Soule Sleeper* — *Anabaptist* — *Familist* — *Secker* — *Diuorcer*

about the country, preaching. Just as strange were the Ranters, a sect which believed that there was no such thing as sin, and that everything, including wives, ought to be shared. These Ranters were imprisoned if they preached in public, for their teaching was thought to be dangerous and immoral.

Such were the sects which flourished and whose teachings you could hear on Sundays when Cromwell ruled England. None of them would have been allowed to preach while Charles I had been on the throne, but few ordinary people felt that they were any better off for this new freedom. They would rather be allowed to do as they pleased in their own homes without being informed against and fined. 'Pish,' said one old soldier, who had actually fought against the King, 'let religion alone; give me my small liberty.'

Military government

Cromwell knew full well that he was disliked. He was once asked how he could carry on when nine out of ten men were against him. His answer was another question: 'What if I put a sword into the tenth man's hand?' Thus, when all else failed, he divided up the country and put an army officer in charge of each area. This was not only very unpopular; it was also very expensive. A new tax called the assessment had to be introduced and was soon bringing in £1,440,000 a year. This was much more than any king had ever asked for, let alone been granted, but the government still needed more. Ruling under such circumstances was a thankless task for Cromwell. The only thing which gave him

A selection of religious sects from a broadsheet of 1647.

strength to go on was the conviction that he was doing God's will. If he allowed the people their way, he knew they would want Charles II on the throne, and Cromwell was certain that God had not allowed the monarchy to be abolished just for it to be brought back again.

Cromwell's death

So Cromwell ruled on, isolated and unpopular, until 1658 when, after a short illness, he died. He was a remarkable man. A respectable country gentleman, he had risen to be ruler of England. People have always argued about his merits, and always will. A splendid soldier, he made England feared and respected abroad, but was less successful in domestic politics. His policies were sensible, and often ahead of his time. Freedom of worship, fair and efficient government, cheap justice and education for all are aims which all would approve. The trouble was that Cromwell was unable to find anybody other than the army to co-operate with him in governing, and the army was universally detested.

The Protector was buried with great ceremony. John Evelyn saw his funeral and wrote of him lying 'in a velvet bed of state, drawn by six horses clad in velvet'. The body was clothed 'in royal robes, crowned with a crown, and with sceptre and orb like a King'. Yet, in spite of all the pomp, Evelyn thought it 'the joyfullest funeral that ever I saw, for there was none that cried but dogs, which the soldiers hooted away with a barbarous noise, drinking and taking tobacco in the streets as they went'. It was the beginning of the end of the republic.

The Restoration

For more than a year after Cromwell died there was chaos. To begin with, his son Richard became Lord Protector in his place, but he had no wish to govern and soon retired. Then the Parliament which Cromwell had turned out in 1653 was brought back, but this only made matters worse than ever, with the army leaders quarrelling with

A gentleman 'taking tobacco' in a long clay pipe. Such pipes were in use for more than 200 years. They broke very easily and bits of them are frequently dug up in gardens and fields.

each other and with the Parliament. There seemed no way to get a government which would work, and which everybody would accept. The deadlock was broken by General George Monk, who commanded the army which Cromwell had sent to look after Scotland. He was a shrewd, commonsense, down-to-earth man, very popular with his troops, who would trust and obey him, whatever he told them to do. Early in 1660, he decided to come down to London, with his army, and as he came, he tried to find out what sort of government the people of the country wanted. There was only one answer. They wanted a king and parliament, as they had had before.

Monk and his army were able to overcome all opposition and on 29 May 1660, Charles II entered London. Evelyn described the scene:

He came with a triumph of over twenty thousand horse and foot brandishing their swords and shouting with unexpressible joy. The ways were strewn with flowers, the bells were ringing, the streets were hung with tapestry, and the fountains were running wine. The Mayor, Aldermen and all the Companies, in their chains of gold, liveries, and banners, were present; also the lords and nobles. Everybody was clad in cloth of silver, gold and velvet; the windows and balconies were all set with ladies, trumpets and music, and myriads of people flocked the streets as far as Rochester, so that they took seven hours to pass through the city. I stood in the Strand and beheld it and blessed God. And all this was done without one drop of blood shed and by that very army that had rebelled against him.

A painting by Isaac Fuller of Charles II's triumphant return to Whitehall Palace in 1660. On the extreme right is the Banqueting Hall, outside which his father had been executed.

England was a monarchy once again.

In 1656 a few coins showing Cromwell's head were struck. This is a gold broad, worth twenty shillings.

Dates to remember

1646 Final defeat of the King
1649 Execution of King
1653 Cromwell became Protector
1658 Death of Cromwell
1660 Restoration of Charles II

Things to do

1 Try to find out if any Civil War battles were fought in your neighbourhood. If so, try to find out about them in the local library. You might be able to visit the site, and work out what happened, or be able to write an account of it with plans of how the armies moved.

2 Try to find out some more about the various sorts of cannon mentioned by Cromwell in his letter after the battle of Naseby.

3 Write a few pages of an informer's diary.

4 Is there a Quaker Meeting House in your district? If so, find out when the meeting was established.

Things to discuss

1 Was the trial and execution of Charles I right? If not, what else could have been done with him?

2 Which of the two estimates of Cromwell, below, do you think nearer the truth?

First, the opinion of the Earl of Clarendon, a Royalist.

In a word, as he had all the wickedness against which damnation is denounced and for which Hell fire is prepared, so he had some virtues, and he will be looked upon by posterity as a brave bad man.

Now see what a member of his own household, John Maidston, thought of him.

A larger soul, I think, hath seldom dwelt in a house of clay than his was. He lived and died in comfortable communion with God. He sought the welfare of his people and spake peace to his seed.

Books to read

M. Blakeway, *A Roundhead Soldier,* Oxford University Press
John Buchan, *A Book of Escapes* (Chapter on Charles II), Nelson
E. Garnett, *The Civil War,* Black
J. L. Davies (ed.), *The English Civil War,* Cape (Jackdaw)
J. L. Davies (ed.), *The Trial and Execution of Charles I,* Cape (Jackdaw)
J. Wroughton, *Cromwell and the Roundheads,* Macmillan
E. Murphy, *Cavaliers and Roundheads,* Longmans
P. Rush, *Strange Stuarts* (Chapter on Gerrard Winstanley), Hutchinson
R. R. Sellman, *Civil War and Commonwealth,* Methuen
R. Sutcliffe, *Heroes and History* (Chapter on Montrose), Batsford

Chapter 4
Charles II 1660–85

The Merry Monarch

The new King, Charles II, aged thirty, was very different from his father. He was tall and dark, casual and easy-going. While Charles I had always been serious, Charles II was constantly teasing and mocking in a gentle, sarcastic way. He was quick-witted and intelligent, and could always answer a difficult question with an appropriate jest. He had a very poor opinion of human nature and never really trusted any of his ministers. Yet he seemed to understand the people whom he ruled better than did any of his advisers. He had few ambitions, but was determined, as he put it, 'not to go on his travels again'.

The Declaration of Breda

Although the country was pleased to see Charles back, people did not want to go back to the days before 1641, when the King had so much power. Charles knew this, and before he came to England, he had issued the Declaration of Breda, in which he had promised to allow freedom

Charles II was far from handsome, as this portrait by John Riley shows.

The pomp and splendour of Charles II's coronation in Westminster Abbey. Somewhere in the congregation sat Samuel Pepys, who described the ceremony in his diary.

THE CORONATION OF CHARLES THE II IN WESTMINSTER ABBEY THE 23 OF APRIL 1661

of worship and let Parliament decide who, if anyone, should be punished for rebelling against his father. In addition, Parliament was to settle the country's finances. Thus the Civil War had not been fought in vain. Charles himself would have liked to increase the power of the monarchy, but he was not prepared to risk his throne to do it.

The Restoration settlement

For the first few years of his reign, Charles had few problems. A new Parliament had been called in 1661, and it was so loyal that it would do almost anything for him. What was more, he had an honest and hardworking minister, a worthy old lawyer, the Earl of Clarendon. He was often rather irritating, for he lectured Charles when he neglected business, or gave money to some worthless man or woman, but Charles bore it all with great good humour. He knew that Clarendon would set the country to rights, and indeed, within five years all was settled. First the army was paid off and disbanded – which relieved everybody. Then Parliament re-established the Church of England, complete with bishops and prayer book, with all its old power and authority. In addition, all other forms of worship were forbidden. Neither Charles, who had great sympathy with the Catholics, nor Clarendon liked this after what had been promised at Breda, but they decided to let Parliament have their way. After all, Parliament had voted the King more than £1,000,000 a year, which was more than his father had ever had, though it was much less than Cromwell had needed to run the country.

The fall of Clarendon

The first big change came in 1667. For years Clarendon had been unpopular with almost everybody. Many were irritated by the way in which he preached at people. Others believed him to be dishonest and ambitious. For instance, he sold Dunkirk, captured by Cromwell, to

A French engraving of Dunkirk, with its elaborate channel and fortifications. They were much too expensive for England to maintain.

It is easy to see why Londoners were jealous of Clarendon House. It was a fine building costing £50,000. On his fall Clarendon sold it to General Monk, by then Duke of Albemarle. It stood near the present Piccadilly Circus.

the French, and his enemies claimed that he pocketed part of the price to help pay for a mansion he was having built. Indeed, they even went so far as to christen it 'Dunkirk House'. Many also disliked the fact that his daughter had married the King's brother, James, Duke of York, a Catholic. They were even more angry when Charles's queen, Catherine of Braganza, a Portuguese princess, failed to produce an heir to the throne, for this meant that on Charles's death James would become King, and Clarendon's daughter would be Queen. Some even said that Clarendon had known that Catherine could have no children when he arranged the marriage.

Now none of these accusations was true, for Clarendon was far too honest to stoop to lying and cheating, but this did not prevent a storm of complaints being raised against him which came to a head when the English did very badly in a war against the Dutch. At last, Parliament accused him of treason, and Charles was faced with the choice between

Shaftesbury in his Lord Chancellor's robes. He was a frail man, who was often ill and in pain. He had an internal ulcer which was drained through a silver tap in his side.

defying Parliament and betraying Clarendon. He did not hesitate. He could get another adviser, and one who would be less tiresome than Clarendon, but he would never be able to get another Parliament as good as the one elected in 1661. He therefore packed Clarendon off into exile, and took over the direction of the government himself, helped by five advisers, the ablest of whom was Anthony Ashley Cooper, first Earl of Shaftesbury, a man with great organizing ability, huge ambition, and great daring.

The Secret Treaty of Dover   1670

Almost at once, Charles's policies altered. The country had had time to settle down. Now was the time to try to increase his power and grant freedom of worship. But first he needed an ally in case anything went wrong. There seemed to be only one, the young King of France, Louis XIV. Fortunately for Charles, the one person in the world he really trusted completely, his sister Henrietta, was married to Louis XIV's brother. Using her as his envoy, Charles began negotiations, and in 1670 signed a secret treaty at Dover, by which he promised to go to war against Holland and declare himself a Catholic. In return Louis promised him £160,000 and the help of French troops in case of trouble. With France as his ally, Charles now felt he could go on. He therefore declared war on Holland, and in 1672, without consulting Parliament he issued a Declaration of Indulgence which granted freedom of worship to everybody. The result was a storm of protest. The fact that the Queen and the King's brother were both Catholics, the Declaration of Indulgence and the war against Holland, combined to make people suspicious. Parliament refused to grant the King any money until he withdrew his declaration. What was more, they passed a Test Act, which said that only members of the Church of England could hold any government posts – including commissions in the army and navy. Charles's policy had failed.

Whigs and Tories

He had, moreover, offended Shaftesbury, who had not been told all the King's plans. From 1673 onwards, this crafty politician was working against Charles, building up a party in Parliament to oppose him, and organizing political clubs up and down the country. Not to be outdone, Charles got a new minister, Lord Danby, to do the same for him, and soon there were two parties in Parliament. The one, organized by Danby to support Charles, was called the Court Party. Its opponents, claiming that all supporters of the court must be Catholic sympathizers, called them Tories, after a gang of wild Irish rebels.

Shaftesbury's party was called the Country Party, to show that they got their support not from the court, but from the country at large. Their opponents called them Whigs, after a group of wild republicans in Scotland. The names stuck for 200 years, long after their origin was forgotten. Shaftesbury, supported by the Puritans, who were disappointed that the Church of England had been given back its old power, had the majority of the Commons on his side, but Charles could usually rely on the Lords. Meanwhile, he had to give up all idea of carrying on with the policy he had started in 1672. It was far too dangerous. All that he could do was to try to keep friendly with France in case things got worse, and hope that Shaftesbury would do something stupid. But Shaftesbury was very cunning and popular, and his hold on Parliament seemed to grow stronger rather than weaker.

No Popery!

The real crisis for Charles came in 1678, and it began quietly enough. One day a very strange pair of men might have been seen going to visit a London magistrate, Sir Edmund Berry Godfrey, to lay some information before him. One of them, Israel Tonge, was a poor mad Protestant clergyman, who had been convinced for years that the Catholics were plotting to destroy the Protestant religion in England. His head was always buzzing with plots, and nobody took him seriously.

The devil in this caricature provided the Pope with plotters, like Coleman and the rest.

His companion was a stranger. He was an extraordinary looking man, shortish and thickset, with a large head and a chin so long that it was remarked that his mouth seemed to be in the middle of his face! His voice was high and whining, and he spoke in a drawling, affected way. His name was Titus Oates, and he had come to Sir Edmund, perhaps the most respected magistrate in London, to tell him of a Catholic plot to kill the King and put the Duke of York on the throne. The very idea seemed fantastic, but then it was no less likely than the Gunpowder Plot, and Oates told such a convincing story, so full of detail, that Sir Edmund was bewildered and uncertain.

But the magistrate was not the only person to have been told of the plot. Tonge and Oates had spread their story all over London, and soon the Council asked for details. Oates gave them. For two whole days he sat before the Council, telling them how he had pretended to be a Catholic, and had been admitted to a Jesuit college, where he had heard of a plot, hatched by the Pope, Louis XIV and every prominent Catholic in England. Charles was to be murdered, James made King, the citizens of London were to be massacred as they slept, and everybody was to be forced to become Catholic, or die. Some of the Council were doubtful, but Oates seemed to know all the details. 'If he be a liar', wrote one of them, 'he is the greatest and adroitest I ever saw.' In the end, they invited Charles himself to come and hear the story. Charles listened, but was not impressed. When Oates named Lord Bellasis as one of the commanders of the Catholic forces in England, he even laughed out loud, for Lord Bellasis had been bedridden for years. Moreover, he caught Oates out in a lie, for Titus claimed that a member of the Spanish Royal family he had seen was tall and dark, while Charles knew him to be short and fair. But Oates brazened it out, and though Charles said that he did not believe him, the Council did, and decided to act on his story.

Sir Edmund dies

First, they began to arrest those Catholics whom Oates had accused, and they found that one of them, Father Coleman, employed by the Duke of York, had written indiscreet letters to Catholics on the Continent, and copies of these were found. The Council jumped to the conclusion that Oates was right, and ordered Coleman to be brought to trial. Even more important, Sir Edmund Berry Godfrey disappeared from his home and then, to the horror of all, was found strangled and stabbed in a ditch. To this day nobody can be sure of how he died, but rumours immediately began to circulate. Soon witnesses came forward and claimed to have seen the murder done. Three innocent Catholics were tried for his murder, found guilty and hanged. By now, London was in a tumult. Oates was hailed as Saviour of the Nation, Coleman was hanged, drawn and quartered for high treason and Catholics were arrested on all sorts of charges. To be on the safe side, even the cellars of the House of Lords were searched regularly.

S.r E.B.Godfree takeing D.r Oates his depositions.

Playing cards illustrate various incidents in the Popish Plot. *Above:* Oates gives his evidence to Sir Edmund Berry Godfrey. *Below:* he repeats it to the King and Council.

D.r Oates discovereth y̆ Plot to y̆ King and Councell.

Coleman drawn to his execution.

Above: Father Coleman is drawn to his execution. *Below:* the execution of five Catholic priests for plotting to murder the King.

The Execution of the 5 Iesuitts.

Exclusion for James

In all this excitement, two men kept their heads. One was Shaftesbury. He decided to direct this great wave of anti-Catholic feeling so that it would sweep the Catholic, James, Duke of York, out of the line of succession to the throne. He therefore introduced a bill into Parliament to prevent James from ever becoming King. If it was dangerous for a Catholic to be an officer in the army, then how much more dangerous it was to allow one to be King! You had only to look at the details of the dreadful plot uncovered by Dr Oates to realize what frightful crimes Catholics would commit. Was it safe to trust the liberties of the country in the hands of a man of such a religion? Many members of the Commons thought it was not.

King Monmouth?

There was, however, one great difficulty. If James was not to be King when Charles died, then who was? It was not an easy question to answer. One solution was that Charles should divorce his wife, marry again and hope that his second wife would have a child who could be brought up as a Protestant. Or, alternatively, there was James's daughter, Mary, who was married to her Protestant cousin, William of Orange. She could perhaps succeed Charles. But Charles refused to divorce his wife and Shaftesbury did not really want Mary or William to rule. He therefore brought forward a third candidate, the illegitimate Duke of Monmouth, the handsome Protestant son of Charles II. Clearly, Monmouth could not succeed to the throne if he was in fact illegitimate, so Shaftesbury claimed that Charles had secretly married the Duke's mother, Lucy Walter, so that the young Duke was really the rightful heir to the throne. So convincing were Shaftesbury's arguments, that he persuaded the House of Commons to pass the bill excluding James from the throne, but it was rejected by the Lords.

Meanwhile, Charles too, was calm. So long as everybody was howling for the blood of the Catholics, he did nothing to try to save them. He knew that if he tried to pardon any of them, then Shaftesbury was quite capable of turning the anger of the country against him, King or not. He was not prepared to risk this. Even when the eighty-year-old Earl of Stafford was sentenced to death for treason he allowed him to be executed, even though he knew him to be innocent. When the Earl of Essex told him that he believed another victim, Archbishop Plunket of Armagh, was innocent, Charles turned on him and retorted, 'Then, my lord, be his blood on your own conscience. You might have saved him if you would. I cannot pardon him because I dare not.'

On the other hand, Charles dug his heels in firmly when it came to the Exclusion Bill. He steadfastly refused to desert James and would have nothing to do with any suggestion that the Duke of Monmouth had any right to succeed him. He told Shaftesbury, 'I will never yield. The older I grow, the more steadfast I become. I have reason and law in my favour.' Shaftesbury thought he could bully him into giving way, but he could not, for Charles was sure that the majority of Englishmen would prefer James, the rightful heir, to succeed him.

Charles triumphs

Slowly, the tide began to turn. The first sign was when Oates accused the Queen and her doctor of plotting to murder the King. Wakeman, the doctor, was brought for trial before Lord Chief Justice Scroggs. Helping him was Sir George Jeffreys, and the chief witness against Wakeman was Oates himself. This was a combination that had been the death of many Catholics, but, to the astonishment of all, Wakeman was found not guilty, for Oates's evidence was torn to shreds by the judge. Charles decided that the time had come to act. He therefore called a new Parliament to meet at Oxford. Normally Parliament met at London, but Shaftesbury had got such a hold over the London mob, that Charles decided it would be safer if it met somewhere else. He chose Oxford because it had always been a very loyal city. When Parliament met, Shaftesbury at once introduced an Exclusion Bill, and Charles, after only three days, dissolved Parliament and never called another. Shaftesbury tried to rouse the country to rebellion, but failed. He realized the game was up and fled to Holland, where he died. Meanwhile, Oates was imprisoned.

The end of Charles's reign

For the last four years of his reign, Charles ruled in peace. He had enough money to do without Parliament, because the taxes granted in 1661 were now bringing in much more money. He was also given money by Louis XIV. It may seem strange that one King should pay another in this way, but it was well worthwhile to Louis, for he knew that if Charles turned against him and called Parliament it would probably want to go to war against France. It was cheaper to pay Charles than to fight the whole country. Meanwhile Charles, now middle-aged, was content to work quietly at loosening the hold that the Whigs had gained on the election machinery. Some day, in his own good time, he might want to call another Parliament and he was determined that if he did it should be a loyal one. He no longer had any thought of trying to grant freedom of worship. He had learned from the events of 1672 that the country was not ready for it. It was best to let sleeping dogs lie. Only one thing worried him. What would his brother James do when he became King? He was such an obstinate man, and so fervent a Catholic that Charles feared the worst.

Titus Oates in the pillory. When James II became king, Oates was sentenced to be whipped twice through London, imprisoned for life and to stand in the pillory every year.

The first copper coins carrying a portrait of the king were struck in Charles II's reign. They were made from copper imported from Sweden.

Dates to remember

1660   The Restoration of Charles II
1670   The Secret Treaty of Dover
1673   The Test Act

Things to do

1 Read the following extract from a letter written by Charles II to his sister, then answer the questions printed below it.

> Whitehall, May 7th
>
> To Madame,
>
>   I have so often asked your pardon for omitting to write to you, as I am almost ashamed to do it now. The truth is, the last week I absolutely forgot it till it was too late, for I was at the Duchess of Richmond's, who, you know, I have not seen this twelve months, and she put it out of my head it was post day.
>
>   I am sure the suddeness of your recovery is as near a miracle as anything can be. And though you find yourself very well now, for God's sake have a care of your diet, and believe the plainer your diet is the better health you will have.
>
>   I ask Pardon for forgetting to deliver your message to James, but I have done it now. He shall answer for himself, and I am sure he has no excuse, if he does fail in writing, I fear he takes a little after his father.

(a) Where was Charles's sister living?
(b) Who was the 'James' referred to in the last paragraph?
(c) What does the letter tell us about Charles's character?

2 Try to get hold of pictures of Clarendon and Danby.

Things to discuss

Why did people believe Titus Oates?

Books to read

M. C. Borer, *Famous Rogues* (Chapter on Colonel Blood) Longmans
P. Rush, *Strange Stuarts* (Chapter on Titus Oates), Hutchinson

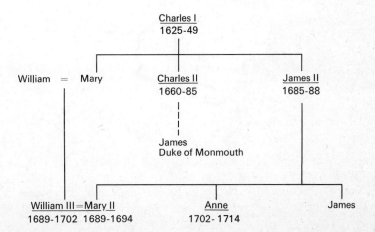

Family tree of Charles I's descendants. The dotted line shows that Monmouth was illegitimate.

Chapter 5
James II and the Revolution of 1688

James's fears

In 1685, Charles had a fit and died only a few days later. On his death-bed he kept the promise he had made fifteen years earlier, and declared himself a Catholic. He died leaving the country as a whole quiet, united and contented; but James, now fifty-one years old, was none the less worried. He thought that because he was a Catholic many Englishmen did not want him to be King. After all, it was not long since Titus Oates had as good as accused him of treason and the House of Commons had passed a bill excluding him from the throne. What was more, James set himself a difficult task, for he was determined to give all Englishmen, even Catholics and Quakers, the right to worship as they pleased. He feared that it might be impossible to persuade the country to accept this, for Catholics in particular were still very unpopular, but he felt that this was his duty. Even if he was doomed to fail, he was determined to do his best, however powerful his opponents, or how-ever hopeless the situation. If he could give his fellow-Catholics equal rights with everybody else, it was, he felt, worth risking his throne, or even his life.

Monmouth's rebellion

Not that James had very high hopes. Indeed, he thought it very likely that the country would rise against him, as it had risen against his father. All that he could do was to try to be prepared when the rising came. In fact, rebellion came before he had been on the throne a year,

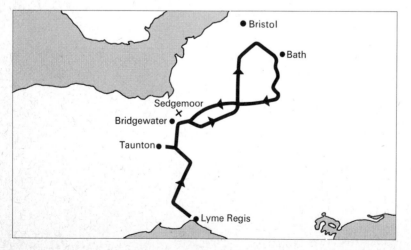

Monmouth's march around the West Country. At one point he decided to attack Bristol, but withdrew because the defences of the city looked too strong. His search for recruits caused his apparently aimless wanderings.

A print of the Battle of Sedgemoor showing the ditch which stopped Monmouth's advance. In fact it was wider than this – and much longer. Compare the weapons of the rival armies.

The fate awaiting some of the rebels captured by the royal army.

before he had done anything which could possibly upset anybody. This rebellion, which broke out in Dorset and Somerset, Shaftesbury's country, was led by the Protestant Duke of Monmouth, who once more claimed to be the rightful heir to Charles II. He had himself proclaimed King at Taunton, and tried to raise an army. To his dismay he found that none of the gentry would join him, but he managed to get together an army of about 6,000 countrymen, most of whom were badly armed and had no experience of fighting. He then went around the west, trying to get new recruits, but as fast as new men joined, others left to go back to their homes and families.

Meanwhile, James had ordered his army to go down to the west to crush the rising. They made their way to Somerset, and camped on a piece of flat land, once marsh, but now drained by huge ditches. The name of the place is Sedgemoor. Here, as they lay in camp, they were attacked by Monmouth's army. Monmouth had hoped that his attack would be a complete surprise, but unfortunately for him his men found their way blocked by one of the drainage ditches, and the Royal army had time to get to arms. Better armed and equipped, furnished with plenty of cavalry, and all trained soldiers, they made short work of Monmouth's men. Soon, all over the west cowering runaways, among them Monmouth himself, were crouching in ditches to escape the vengeance of the Royal troops, who tended to hang first, and ask questions afterwards.

Portrait of Jeffreys when he was Recorder of London. He made his name in the Popish Plot trials, and became Lord Chief Justice at the age of thirty-eight.

Monmouth's execution on Tower Hill. Note the hearse on the right.

The Bloody Assize

Once the rebellion was crushed, James decided to make an example of the rebels to discourage any others who might think of making trouble. He therefore sent the Lord Chief Justice, Judge Jeffreys, to the west to try those rebels who had been captured and imprisoned. Monmouth himself, found in a ditch, was brought to London for trial, condemned, and executed. His followers, herded together in overcrowded prisons or, where these were too small, even crammed into churches, awaited the arrival of Judge Jeffreys. Now Jeffreys was a very able man, with an excellent knowledge of the law, but he was also by nature quick-tempered and violent. He was, moreover, suffering agonies from a stone in his bladder, which made him almost mad with pain. So far as he was concerned, the quicker the trials were over, the better. There was no doubt that the prisoners were guilty of high treason, for they had fought at Monmouth's side at Sedgemoor. Rebellion was a crime which filled the judge with horror, and he was quite sure that all rebels deserved the dreadful penalty of hanging, drawing and quartering. Most of his fellow-countrymen agreed with him. What they did dislike in Jeffreys, however, was the violence of his language and his bullying of witnesses and juries alike if they did not agree with him. He went from centre to centre, trying the rebels in batches. With him came the executioner, and in the end, about 200 were hanged. A thousand others were transported to the colonies as slaves. This assize is usually known as the Bloody Assize, and Jeffreys is often looked upon as a sort of monster, perhaps rather unfairly. It was, after all, James's responsibility that so many men were put on trial.

You might expect the harsh punishment of the rebels to make James unpopular, but it did not seem to at the time. What is certain, however, is that the rebellion frightened him. He decided that it would be best to keep a large army in constant readiness in case there was another. But an army is no good if you cannot trust the officers, and James feared that Protestant officers might not serve him faithfully. He therefore decided to appoint Catholics. The only trouble was that this was against the law. To get round this, James claimed that he had the right to ignore the law in such cases if he chose, and when a case was brought to trial, the judges agreed with him. He was therefore able to go on appointing Catholics to important positions in the army, which he stationed on Hounslow Heath, near London.

The seven bishops

Feeling more secure now, James decided he could try granting the freedom of worship which lay so near to his heart. To do this, he issued a declaration, similar to that issued by Charles II in 1672. This declaration suspended all those laws which laid down what religion people had to follow. He then waited for the reaction. None came. His declaration was ignored. James tried again, but this time he ordered that his declaration should be read in churches. There was certainly a reaction this

Those rebels who were tried by Jeffreys were hanged with rather more formality than those hanged by the army without trial.

67

time! Seven bishops, including the Archbishop of Canterbury, presented him with a petition, in which they claimed that the declaration was illegal. James was shocked. Up to that time, all through the seventeenth century, whoever else had attacked the monarchy, the Church of England had always stood firm. Now the very bishops had turned against him. Determined that they must be punished for their disloyalty, James ordered them to be brought to trial on a charge of publishing a document liable to encourage rebellion.

Their trial provoked nation-wide interest. On the day the verdict came out, James was inspecting his army on Hounslow Heath. Suddenly, he heard cheers ringing out from all parts of the camp. Startled, he asked what all the excitement was about, and was told that his troops had just heard that the seven bishops had been found not guilty. James was deeply shocked at the verdict, but most Englishmen were delighted, for it showed that James, in spite of his army, could not do as he pleased with an English jury.

The country's fears

The plain fact was that the English nation was now just as nervous of James as he was of them. At the beginning of his reign, they had mostly been prepared to overlook his religion and accept him as their king without question. Now they were not so sure. They feared that James really intended to convert the whole country to the Roman Catholic religion, and that he was prepared to use force if need be. What other explanation was there for his keeping an army with Catholic officers? In addition, James had shown that he was not prepared to allow laws to stand in his way. He seemed to think that all he had to do was to issue a declaration setting aside an Act of Parliament, and that was that. At that rate, nothing was safe. People began to recall what their parents had told them about the Gunpowder Plot and remember what they had read of the sufferings of Protestants under Queen Mary Tudor. What

A Dutch engraving showing the seven bishops being greeted enthusiastically as they are taken to the Tower in a barge.

The seven bishops became national heroes. *Centre:* the Archbishop of Canterbury. Above him are the bishops of St Asaph and Ely, flanking him the bishops of Chichester, and of Bath and Wells, below him the bishops of Peterborough and Bristol.

was to prevent James burning Protestants at the stake, as she had done? Perhaps this was his real aim. After all, it was well known that James admired Louis XIV, and Louis had just made the Protestant religion illegal in France.

Meanwhile, members of the nobility were nervous too. Where would James stop? He had already promoted Catholics to many important positions in the state. Might he perhaps make Catholicism the official religion and dismiss all his Protestant advisers? Might he even try to get back for the Church those lands, now mostly in the hands of the nobility, which Henry VIII had taken from it? Only one thing held them back from rebellion. This was James's age, for in 1688 he was already fifty-five, the age at which his brother Charles had died. True, he still enjoyed excellent health, but he could not be expected to live much longer and, when he died, he would be succeeded by his daughter Mary, who was a Protestant, married to William of Orange, himself a great Protestant leader. So, however nervous they might be, the nobility waited patiently, hoping for James's early death, and keeping in touch with William in Holland.

The revolution of 1688

Then on 10 June, all their calculations were upset when James's queen, the young Mary of Modena, whom he had married when his first wife died, gave birth to a son. Now their hopes of James being succeeded by a Protestant were destroyed at a blow. His son was certain to be brought up as a Catholic and would carry on James's policy. They decided to act, and invited William to come to England with an army at his back. William accepted, set sail, and landed at the little Devon fishing port of Brixham on 5 November. James made his way with an army to Salisbury to meet him, but then changed his mind and went back to London. The truth was that he did not know what to do for the best, and so did nothing. James felt alone and deserted. He sent his wife and son over to France, then followed them himself, leaving his throne for William, without striking a blow in its defence.

James's reign is rather a pathetic story. He tried hard to do what he believed to be right and really seems to have wanted to give everybody the right to worship as they thought fit. But he was so frightened of rebellion, and took so many precautions, that he made his people suspicious and frightened, and thus drove them to rebellion.

James's flight left the game in William's hands. Soon he was in London. But he was not really his own master. He had no right to be King of England. James was still alive, and had a son. What was more, even if you ignored them, then it was William's wife, Mary, who should have ruled and not William himself. It was some time before Parliament could get round this difficulty, but in the end the Commons and Lords agreed that James had exceeded his power as King. They said he had no right to do away with laws as he had done, and concluded that they were justified in deposing him. They also claimed that they had the

William III and Mary.

William and Mary embarking for England. The surrounding ships are firing salutes.

right to offer the throne to whoever they thought fit. Many members wished the crown to go to Mary who was, after all, James's daughter, but William would have none of it. He had not come to England, he said, to be his wife's 'gentleman usher'. Eventually, Parliament solved the problem by offering the throne to William and Mary jointly, each of them to have equal power. They accepted. The revolution was over. Often called the 'Glorious Revolution', it established, without a drop of blood being shed, that Parliament and the law were of more account than the wishes of the monarch.

William III

William III's position as King was much weaker than that of any of those who had come before him in the seventeenth century. He did not rule because he had inherited the throne, as they had done, but because a group of powerful nobles had invited him over and because Parliament had approved of him as King. If they had not thought he would do as they wished, he would not have been King and if at any time he was tempted to do anything which they did not like, he knew full well that they might get rid of him and replace him by somebody else. Moreover, he was never popular. Many suspected him because he was a foreigner, and others did not like his cold, suspicious manner. However much people might admire the determination with which he overcame his persistent ill health, they felt that there was something almost inhuman about him. Thus when his popular wife Mary died in 1694, William was left very much on his own. Fortunately, he was sensible enough to understand the position and, even though he did not like having to do what Parliament and the nobility wanted, he was careful not to go directly against their wishes.

The Bill of Rights

But Parliament did not just trust to the King's common sense to prevent him from doing anything foolish. They also insisted on him agreeing to a 'Bill of Rights', which took away the King's power to suspend laws as James had done, made a standing army illegal, and declared that Parliaments should be called frequently. In addition, the judges were put under the control of Parliament so that the King could no longer dismiss them if he disagreed with their decisions. Later, another act was passed saying that Parliament had to be dissolved every three years and a new one called. This was to prevent the King keeping a Parliament which he liked for a long time, as Charles II had done. To make sure that Parliament met at least every year, enough money was only voted for one year's government at a time, and even when it was found necessary to raise an army it was only made legal for twelve months at a time. In all these ways, Parliament made sure that the King could not do as he pleased.

The Toleration Act 1689

So far as religion was concerned, the Church of England lost some of its power. Some of the bishops had supported James II, while the Whigs who had invited William over tended to support the Nonconformists. As a result, a Toleration Act was passed to allow freedom of worship for Nonconformists. It was still not legal for them to hold any official positions, but many of them did and later an act was passed each year forgiving them for breaking the law. No such act was passed for Roman Catholics, however. Memories of the Popish Plot and James II were too recent for that.

The end of the struggle

By 1689, the solutions had been found for the two problems which had confronted the monarchy since 1603. By the Toleration Act, the Puritans had been granted freedom of worship, and never lost it again. So far as politics were concerned, Parliament was now in a position where

This James II halfpenny was made from Cornish tin, to encourage local industry. Each coin contained a copper plug to make it more difficult to forge.

it could actually decide who should be king. This was a far cry from the days when James I and Charles I had maintained that they had a God-given right to do as they pleased, without even consulting Parliament. In fact, after 1689, the King could no longer do anything with which the House of Commons disagreed. He had to learn to keep on good terms with them.

As William and Mary ruled jointly, both their heads had to appear on coins until Mary's death in 1694.

Dates to remember

1685   Death of Charles II
         Monmouth's rebellion
1688   William III landed

Things to do

1   Read the following extract from a letter written by James II to one of his generals, and then answer the questions printed below it.

Things being come to that extremity that I have been forced to send away the Queen and my son the Prince of Wales that they might not fall into the enemy's hands, which they must have done had they stayed, I am obliged to do the same thing, and endeavour to secure myself the best I can, in hopes it will please God, out of His infinite mercy to this unhappy nation, to touch their hearts with true loyalty and honour. If I could have relied upon all my troops I might not have been put to this extremity I am in, and would at least have had one blow for it; but though I know there are many loyal and brave men amongst you, yet you know you yourself, and several of the general officers told me, it was no ways advisable to venture myself at their head. There remains nothing more for me but to thank you and all those officers and soldiers who have stuck to me and been truly loyal.

(a)   What was happening when this letter was written?
(b)   What reason did James give for not trying to fight?
(c)   What does this letter tell us of James's character?

2   Try to get hold of pictures of James II and Monmouth.
3   What is an assize court? Find out which is the assize town for your own district and how often assizes are held there today.

Books to read

F. Grice, *Rebels and Fugitives* (Chapter on Monmouth), Batsford

D. Johnson (ed.), *The Monmouth Rebellion*, Cape (Jackdaw)

B. L. Picard, *The Tower and the Traitors* (Chapter on Monmouth), Batsford

Chapter 6
Restoration London

The town itself

In Restoration times, London was a big town, even by modern standards. It had a population of about 500,000, about the size of Edinburgh or Leeds today. For the England of Charles II, it was enormous; more than ten times as big as Norwich or Bristol, the largest provincial towns. To get any idea of what it looked like, you must forget the tall buildings, raised pavements and wide streets of today's cities and, instead, imagine a town of narrow streets paved with round cobblestones. Often there are no pavements and a single gutter runs down the middle of the road. On each side of the street stand timber-frame houses, most of them a hundred years old or more. Each floor projects a bit over the one below, so that at the top the house almost meets that on the other side of the street. This makes the road very dark, and, to make it more unpleasant, all the refuse from the houses is thrown into the gutter, where it lies until it is cleared up by the street cleaners. They put it in great heaps just outside the city to rot. In the meantime it lies in the middle of the road, providing food for thousands of black rats and millions of flies. Nor is the air clean, for London is an industrial town and the fires of the soap-boilers, dyers, brewers and lime-burners make a 'horrid smoke' over the city.

A foreigner's impression

This smoke particularly impressed foreigners. One of them wrote that London was

a large, yet a very ugly town, pestered with hackney coaches and insolent car-men, shops and tavern's noise, and such a cloud of sea coal as, if there be a resemblance of hell upon earth, it is in this volcano on a foggy day. This pestilent smoke, which corrodes the very iron, and spoils all the moveables, leaving a soot upon all things which it lights, and so fatally seizing upon the lungs of the inhabitants that the cough and consumption spare no man. I have been in a spacious church where I could not discern the minister for the smoke, nor hear him for the people barking.

Of course, there are wider, cleaner streets, and some open spaces with big houses, but these lie outside the old city, and the people who live in them think themselves a cut above those who live in the older part of the town. The King's palace of Whitehall is well away from the slums of the city, though not far enough to escape the smoke and fog altogether.

Typical London houses before the fire of 1666. The one on the corner is more elaborate than the others.

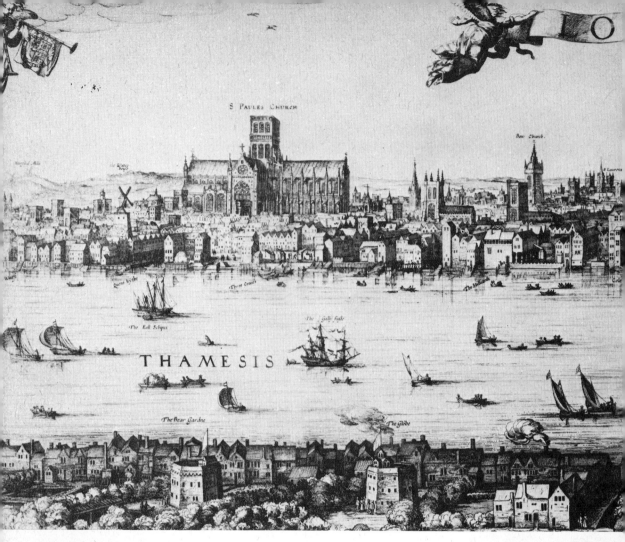

Meet Samuel Pepys

We know quite a lot about living in London in the 1660s because of
Samuel Pepys. Sam, who worked for the government at the Navy Office,
kept a diary. Each day, before he went to bed, he wrote, in shorthand,
an account of what he had done and what he had seen during the day.
As he was a lively, curious man, he did a great deal, and noticed many
interesting things, all of which he recorded in his diary. Being a civil
servant, he had a good deal more money than most people living in
London. He had his own house, and he and his wife, whom he had
married when he was twenty-two and she fifteen, had two or three servants to look after them. His house was not detached, and he had a bit
of trouble when the pit into which his neighbour's lavatory emptied
overflowed into the Pepys's cellar. Apart from this, and some bother with
lazy workmen who came to make alterations, his house did not give him
much trouble.

FLUVIUS

South Warke

London, showing theatres
(foreground), London Bridge,
with its narrow arches covered
with buildings, and *(left)* Old
St Paul's.

Left: portrait of Pepys in 1666.

How he passed his time

His working hours varied a good deal. Usually he started pretty early,
sometimes at six in the morning. He generally travelled by boat, because
the narrow streets made it difficult to get about by road. On one
occasion, when travelling by coach, he knocked a butcher's meat into
the gutter, and had to pay him compensation. There were no such
difficulties on the river. At work he did his best to make sure that the
navy was not being cheated by the contractors who supplied the stores
and food the ships and sailors needed. This was tiring work, and in the
evening Samuel liked to relax. Sometimes he went out with his friends
to a tavern for a drink or two of wine. On such occasions he was liable
to drink too much, and then regret it next morning. Quite often he
went to the theatre, sometimes as often as three or four times a week.
He usually went to see new, fashionable, witty plays about court life,
but sometimes saw one of Shakespeare's plays, which were still being

Above: a drunken crowd at a cock-pit put bets on their favourite birds. The rich man facing us has three £20 notes; one is being stolen.

Left: Nell Gwynne was the most famous actress of Charles II's reign. She bore the king several children.

performed regularly. One great change he noticed in the theatre since it had started up again after the Restoration, was that boys were no longer playing all the female parts. There were now actresses, and Pepys thought this a great improvement.

Of course, he had other amusements too. Being in London he took a great delight in seeing a lot of the life at court, where Charles II was keeping things lively. In addition, like other Londoners, he enjoyed the various fairs which came, with their sideshows and acrobats, at set times of the year. When occasion offered, he would go to watch a public execution, once paying a shilling to stand on a cartwheel to get a better view of the man being hanged. Sometimes he would go to a cockpit to see two fighting cocks set against each other, and perhaps he put a bet on the bird he fancied. At other times he went to prize fights to watch two men fight each other to a standstill, either with bare fists or with more dangerous weapons. Added to this, he was a keen lover of music and often joined with a few friends to sing and play the latest pieces on recorders and virginals. Also he was fond of books, and spent a lot of time and money in St Paul's Churchyard, a great centre for booksellers. Finally, he loved good food and liked to impress his friends with the dishes he provided. One New Year's Day, he gave a breakfast party at which the food consisted of a barrel of oysters, a dish of calves' tongues, a dish of anchovies, wines of all sorts, and Northdown beer.

His clothes

Costumes of the 1660s.

Sam also took a pride in his appearance, liking to keep up with the latest fashion. In 1663, finding that hair powder made his hair 'very foul', he decided to buy one of the new periwigs which were all the rage. He paid £3 for it, which was only £1 less than his cook's wages for the whole year. None of his clothes seem to have been cheap, for that matter. He must have cut a fine figure in his velvet hat, periwig, baize waistcoat faced with lace, black cloth suit faced with red ribbon and silk stockings. When out in London he always carried a sword as well, not for protection, though there were many criminals about, but just for show. He even forgot to use it when he was attacked and bitten by a large savage dog. He tended to spend less money on his wife's clothes, but now and then the 'poor wretch', as he called her, would get a new gown, usually black, or black and white.

His health

Finally, Sam was careful about his health. When he was twenty-five, he had a stone in his gall bladder, which is very painful indeed. In fact it was so agonizing that he decided to have it removed. The operation was successful, and his health was usually fairly good. To keep himself in trim, he carried a hare's foot in his pocket to prevent colic, took a turpentine pill every morning and, when he felt he needed it, went to the surgeon to have some blood let out. Sometimes he had as much as one and three-quarter pints let at once, and always felt the better for it.

One thing he could not do anything about was his eyesight, which gradually got worse from about 1664 onwards, and made him give up his diary in 1669.

The Great Plague 1665

Before he gave up, however, he had written details of the two great disasters which struck London between 1660 and 1670, the Plague of 1665, and the Fire of 1666. Plague, the Pest, or the Black Death, as it was variously called, was nothing new. It had come to Britain first in the Middle Ages and had returned from time to time, especially to London. In the seventeenth century, there had been outbreaks in 1603, 1625 and 1640, but none of them was as bad as the one in 1665.

Symptoms and causes

Plague was a terrible disease, carried by rats and by the fleas which prey on them. Rats were killed by plague, and the fleas left their cooling bodies to find fresh food elsewhere. If a man happened to pass near, they would jump on to him, bite him to feed on his blood, and thus inject the virus of plague into his body. The first the man knew of this was a cold shivering, followed by terrible vomiting, so severe that it sometimes killed. Then came a high fever, which made the patient delirious. There followed the growth of the buboes, black swellings under the armpits and in the groin, which caused great pain. Sometimes these would burst and the fever might then go down, but more often the unfortunate man would be dead before they could do so, killed by the poisoning of his whole body by the germs of plague.

Precautions against plague

In the seventeenth century, the cause of plague was not known and, as a result, the rules they made to try to stop it were not very effective. Let us consider a family of six who lived together in a house, with one of them dead of plague, and another with a high fever. The first thing to be done would be to tell the parish authorities. They would send the Searchers of the Dead, two old women whose job it was to decide the cause of death by looking at the corpse before it was taken away for burial. If they decided that it was a case of plague, then they would tell the authorities. They would send some men to take the sick person to the parish pest house, which was a sort of crude isolation hospital. Often it was only a wooden shed, with a few beds and a doctor in charge.

In the meantime, to prevent the disease spreading, the house would be locked up for forty days, with the other four people inside, and a red cross with the words 'Lord have mercy on us', on the door. Nobody was allowed in or out of the house and, because it had infected rats inside, quite often those left in it caught the disease and died. To escape being shut up, people often bribed the searchers to certify death by plague as being caused by something else, and then left the house. If there were

Inside a plague-stricken house. Four people are ill in bed, while a corpse and an open coffin lie on the floor. The two women with staffs are Searchers of the Dead.

A London street during the plague. Two houses have crosses on their doors. A plague victim is carried to the Pest House in a sedan-chair *(right);* there are two dog killers and two Searchers of the Dead *(centre)*. Open fires burn in the street.

a lot of cases of plague, the authorities took other precautions as well. All the dogs were killed, and public meetings of every kind were forbidden. Finally, to purify the air – for some thought that foul air was a cause of plague – fires were lit in the street outside every sixth house. Needless to say, none of these precautions did any good, for the rats moved as they pleased in and out of the locked houses and, with no dogs to kill them, probably increased in numbers.

Effects of the plague

In 1665, in spite of all that was done, the number of deaths mounted as the weather grew hotter, and went on going up even in the autumn. In the end, over a thousand people in the stricken city were dying of the plague each day. Life in the town came to a standstill. Those who could afford it left London. It is reckoned that about half the population, including the King and all his court, went into the country. Those who

A plague pit outside the city walls. Carts brought the bodies from the city.

were left went about as little as possible. This meant that the streets, usually so busy, were still and quiet, disturbed only occasionally by the screams and groans of the sick and dying. So many died that there was no longer time or room to bury them properly. Instead of orderly funerals in the churchyards by day, with a proper service, the dead, like so much rubbish, were collected each night by a cart. To warn people to be prepared for its coming, the man in charge of it rang a hand bell and shouted 'Bring out your dead'. When the cart was full, it was taken to one of the great plague pits, specially dug outside the city, and the bodies were tipped into it.

Here is part of a letter written by Pepys at the height of the plague.

The absence of the Court and emptiness of the city takes away all occasion of news, save only such melancholy stories as would rather sadden than find your ladyship any divertisement in the hearing; I having stayed in the city till above 7,400 died in one week, and of them above 6,000 of the plague and little noise heard day nor night but tolling of bells; till I could walk Lombard Street and not meet twenty persons from one end to the other and not 50 upon the Exchange; till whole families, 10 and 12 together have been swept away; till my very physician, Dr Burnet, who undertook to secure me against any infection, having survived the month of his own being shut up, died himself of the plague; till the nights though much lengthened, are grown too short to conceal the burials of those that died the day before, people being thereby constrained to borrow daylight for that service: lastly till I could find neither meat nor drink safe, the butcheries being everywhere visited, my brewer's house shut up, and my baker, with his whole family, dead of the plague.

As the weather grew colder with the onset of winter, so the deaths grew less numerous until, by the end of the year, they had almost got back to normal. Nobody can be quite sure how many died of plague that year, but it was probably more than 100,000. The Bill of Mortality for the year, printed on page 214, gives the official figures but it is certainly too small, for it does not include those who were just tipped

Londoners threatened by death (represented by the skeletons) leave their city to take refuge in the country.

into pits without the authorities knowing, or those whose deaths were certified as something different. It was a disaster which has never been forgotten. We still call some people 'pests', and avoid others 'like the plague'.

The Great Fire of 1666

1666 saw London coming back to life. The King returned, the shops reopened, and by September all was back to normal. The epidemic had passed, even though the summer was hot and dry. But in September another disaster, the Great Fire, struck the city. This time it was more or less over in three days. It began at the King's baker's shop in Pudding Lane in the early hours of Sunday, 2 September. Pepys heard of it when his servant Jane, who was working late, called him 'about three in the morning to tell us of a great fire they saw in the City, but I thought it far enough off and so went back to bed again and to sleep'. Later in the day it had a good hold. A Londoner wrote, 'The wind blowing strong eastward, I saw great burning flakes carried up into the air at least three furlongs, these at last landing set on fire houses very remote from each other.' People panicked. The streets were 'full of nothing but people and horses and carts laden with goods ready to run over one another and removing goods from one burned house to another'. As a result 'the engines had no liberty to play, and some of them were tumbled into the river'.

London on fire, showing the extent of the fire, and the flames fanned by the easterly wind.

The spread of the fire

Everybody seemed helpless. Pepys found the Lord Mayor, 'in Canning Street, like a man spent, with a handkerchief about his neck'. He cried 'like a fainting woman "Lord, what can I do? I am spent; people will not obey me. I have been pulling down houses, but the fire overtakes us faster than we can do it."' On Monday the fire continued to spread. On Monday night, when it was at its height, 'you might see in some places whole streets at once in flames that came from the opposite windows,

An advertisement for a fire engine, pumped, as they all were, by hand. If seventeenth-century fire engines had really been as efficient as this, London might not have burned down.

84

which joined into one great flame throughout the whole street; and then you may see the houses tumble, tumble, tumble from one end of the street to the other, with a great crash, leaving the foundations open to the heavens.' There seemed no reason why the fire should not burn on until the whole city was destroyed.

The end of the fire

By Tuesday, the situation was so serious that the King himself intervened, bringing with him his brother, the Duke of York. They 'rode up and down, giving orders for blowing up of houses with gunpowder to make empty spaces for the fire to die in, and standing still to see those orders executed'. On Tuesday night the wind fell, and on Wednesday the fire was stopped, leaving 'a large part of London nothing but stones and rubble, and all exposed to the open air, so that you may see from one end of the city almost to the other.' In all, the fire burned over 13,000 homes and eighty-eight churches, including St Paul's Cathedral. A hundred thousand people were homeless.

Now, come for a walk with John Evelyn, on 7 September 1666.

I went this morning on foot from Whitehall as far as London Bridge, with extraordinary difficulty, clambering over heaps of yet smoking rubbish, and frequently mistaking where I was: the ground under my feet so hot that it even burnt the soles of my shoes. I was infinitely concerned to find that goodly church, St Paul's – now a sad ruin, besides near one hundred more. The lead, iron work, bells, plate etc., melted, all of the Companies' Halls, splendid buildings, arches, entries all in dust; the fountains dried up and ruined, whilst the very waters remained boiling; the voragos of cellars, wells and dungeons, formerly warehouses, still burning in stench and dark clouds of smoke; so that in five or six miles traversing about I did not see one load of timber unconsumed, nor many stones but what were calcined white as snow. The people, who now walked about the ruins, appeared like men in some dismal desert, or rather, in some great city laid waste by a cruel enemy, to which was added the stench that came from some poor creatures' bodies, beds and other combustible goods.

The new London

A huge job of rebuilding had to be done. Several people drew up plans for a completely new city, with straight, wide streets and grand views of fine buildings. The most famous of these was drawn up by Sir Christopher Wren, whose splendid new churches, including St Paul's Cathedral, still stand today. These churches are the only part of Wren's plan which was used, because in the end, they simply built new houses along the lines of the old streets. This was less expensive. There was a difference, though. The government insisted that all the new houses should be built not of timber, but of brick. What was more, they laid down the plans to which they had to be built, and saw to it that the new town had some drains and a proper system of collecting rubbish. This meant that, after 1666, London became a better and healthier city.

St Mary le Bow parish church, designed by Wren after the Fire. His churches are easily recognized by their unconventional spires.

Left: old St Paul's, a huge medieval building with a squat tower, once surmounted by a spire.

Right: new St Paul's, with its great dome, presented a complete break with the old cathedral.

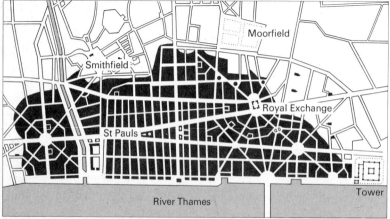

Left: Wren's plan for rebuilding London.

The life of a thief

So much for the changes recorded by Samuel Pepys in his diary. Not everybody in London in the second half of the seventeenth century was as honest and hardworking as he. There were also misfits and criminals, like young John Johnson. He was a thief, and had been one for as long as he could remember. In 1687 he was seventeen years old. He had lived all his life in or near London. He knew nothing of his parents, except that they had 'apprenticed' him to a sweep at the age of four, which was tantamount to being sold into slavery. He had spent the next four years living with the sweep, climbing chimneys to clean them, and stealing odd trinkets from the houses where he had worked. Then, at the age of eight, he had grown too big to be of use to the master sweep, and had been thrown out to fend for himself. Since then, he had lived on his wits. He had run errands and messages, and had worked for anyone who would give him a bed. But he had always been stealing, and for the past two years he had done little else. He stole anything he could lay his hands on, and sold it at a little shop he knew, where the shopkeeper asked no questions so long as the price was right. Of late he had been getting more daring, and had taken to housebreaking.

The police

He had never been caught. He knew London well, and had taken care to learn where the parish boundaries ran. This was important to him because the only police, the Watch, were employed by the parish and would rarely bother to chase a thief once he had left their territory. Indeed, many of them were not really capable of chasing a thief at all, for they were old men, who had taken on the job of patrolling the streets at night because they could get no other. Many of them worked to a regular timetable, patrolling the same street at the same time every night, while others would take a bribe to avoid a certain street at a certain time. Then, if he were discovered, a lively lad could always dodge in and out of all the alleys he knew so well and there was always a friend willing to help against the Watch! John felt pretty sure he would not be caught.

Public hangings

This was just as well, for he knew what would happen to him if he did fall into the hands of the law. He had seen more than one thief hanged; indeed he often went to see executions at Tyburn, which were all in public. Ordinary hangings, when a cart was driven from under the condemned man, and he was left suspended by his neck to strangle, John now found rather dull, but they amazed foreigners. One wrote:

The English laugh at the delicacy of other nations, who make it such a mighty matter to be hanged; their extraordinary courage looks upon it as a trifle. He that is to be hanged first takes care to get himself shaved and handsomely dressed, either in mourning, or in the dress of a bridegroom. This done, he

A London watchman, armed with a staff, and carrying a lamp in the dark streets.

An execution at Tyburn – the modern Marble Arch. The hangman smokes his pipe on top of the gallows, while the prisoner, preceded by a clergyman in a coach, is brought, together with his coffin, in a cart. Clearly the atmosphere is that of a holiday.

sets his friends at work to get him leave to be buried and to carry his coffin with him. When his suit of clothes, his gloves, hat, periwig, nosegay, coffin, flannel dress for his corpse are brought and prepared, the main point is taken care of, his mind is at peace, and then he thinks of his conscience.

Even after the man was dead, the fun was not over.

The bodies and clothes of the dead belong to the executioner; relatives must, if they wish for them, buy them from him, and unclaimed bodies are sold to surgeons to be dissected. You see the most amusing scenes between the people who do not like the bodies to be cut up and the messengers the surgeons have sent for the bodies; blows are given and received. All these scenes are most diverting, and can be witnessed from a sort of amphitheatre erected for the spectators near the gibbet.

But however diverting such scenes were to foreigners, they were everyday to John. He had seen Father Coleman hanged, drawn and quartered for high treason, and had seen the Duke of Monmouth have his head chopped off. He had stood in the cheering crowd which had witnessed Titus Oates being dragged two days running by a cart from one end of London to the other, being whipped all the way, for telling lies on oath. Some days, when he had nothing better to do, John would go along to the stocks or the pillory to see if the cheats and drunks in them were worth throwing at. Sometimes they were, and he amused himself throwing all sorts of refuse and abuse at these helpless men, though once he was prevented from doing so by the fact that the man in the pillory, who was rich, had hired fifty Hackney coaches to stand all round him and protect him.

Murder!

Lately, John had been doing pretty well from his thieving, and reckoned he had earned a night out. Accordingly, he made his way to a tavern, meaning to have a drink or two there. As usual, the drink or two turned out to be many more, and John became quite drunk. Now when drunk, he tended to become violent, and when the tavern keeper refused to serve him any more, he threw his pewter pot at him, and hit him on the temple. The unfortunate man dropped like a stone. He was dead. Immediately, there was a terrible tumult and John, drunk and dazed, was dragged off to the local lock-up. The next day, he was taken before a magistrate, who committed him to Newgate Prison, to await trial at the next assizes.

Prison conditions

Conditions in prisons in the seventeenth century were unbelievable. The cells were dark, damp, overcrowded and insanitary. Most of them were underground.

'In some of those caverns', wrote John Howard, who went visiting prisons in the eighteenth century,

the floor is very damp: in others there is sometimes an inch or two of water: and the straw, or bedding is laid on such floors; seldom on barrack bedsteads. Some jails have no sewers or vaults; and in those that have, if they be not properly attended to, they are, even to a visitant, offensive beyond expression: how noxious then to people constantly confined in those prisons.

It was bad enough for criminals to be confined in conditions like these, but in most places they shared such rooms with debtors as well. Right up until the middle of the nineteenth century, it was possible to be put into prison for failing to pay a debt, however small it might be. What was more, there was no limit to the amount of time you spent in prison – you simply stayed there until you paid the debt. For many, it was impossible to pay unless they left prison and worked, so they stayed there until they died.

Debtors' prisons

In some towns, there were special prisons for debtors, but they were little better than the common jail, unless the debtor had money to spare. If he had, he could rent special accommodation from the jailer, often at very high prices. He could also get better food. The poor debtors, on the other hand, were all crammed together into the worst cells in the prison. Take, for instance, George's Ward, a room sixteen feet by eighteen feet, and eight feet high, in the Fleet Debtors' Prison in London.

A cell in the Fleet Debtors' Prison in London. The jailer on the right is demanding his fees, while the pot boy expects payment for the beer he has brought.

'All last year', reported a committee set up to investigate prison conditions in 1727,

> there were sometimes forty and never less than thirty-two locked up in George's Ward every night. The surface of the room is not enough to contain that number when laid down, so that one half are hung up in hammocks, whilst the other lie on the floor under them. The air is so wasted by the number of persons who breathe in that narrow compass, that it is not sufficient to keep them from stifling, several having in the heat of summer perished for want of air. Every night, at eight of the clock in the winter and nine in the summer, the prisoners are locked up, and from those hours until eight of the clock in the morning in the winter, and five in the summer, they cannot, upon any occasion come out. The stench is noisesome beyond expression.

Some debtors' prisons were worse even than this. Howard described Knaresborough Prison for Town Debtors thus:

> Only one room, about twelve feet square: window seventeen inches by six. Earth floor: no fireplace: very offensive; a common sewer from the town running through it uncovered.

It was no wonder that many prisoners died before they could be brought to trial, and that Howard found, after visiting a prison, that his clothes stank so badly that he could not bear to travel in a closed carriage, but had to go on horseback.

John's trial

John waited about three weeks in Newgate for his trial, and met several people whom he knew there, and talked to them about his case. He could not remember much about what had happened, but he knew that he had not meant to kill the tavern keeper and so intended to plead not guilty. Not that he thought it would do him much good, but there was no harm in trying. Even had he been able to afford it, he was not allowed counsel to defend him, nor was he allowed to give evidence on his own behalf. He could call witnesses if he wished, but they would not be allowed to give evidence on oath. This, according to the prosecution, meant that they were under no obligation to tell the truth, and so should not be believed if what they said contradicted a prosecution witness, who had sworn to tell the truth and was liable to be prosecuted if he lied. He knew, moreover, that everybody in the court would take it for granted that he was guilty. Even the judge was more than likely to help the prosecution. After all, he was employed by the Crown, just as they were, and if he did not think they were presenting their case well enough, he was quite likely to take over from them. Thus everything was weighted against the prisoner. A few hardy souls refused to plead either guilty or not guilty, but in that case they were tied down and heavy weights were piled on them until they died. It was the only torture allowed by English law in ordinary criminal cases. In most countries there were many more.

The fate of those who refused to plead either guilty or not guilty when charged.

A courtroom scene. On the bench sit the judges, beneath them the clerks of the court, the jury *(right)* and the lawyers *(left)*. In the foreground is the prisoner in the dock.

John's trial did not last long. A good deal of the time he did not really understand what was going on. The courtroom was packed with spectators, who had paid for their seats, and they chattered and laughed so much that the lawyers and the judge had difficulty in making themselves heard. John was allowed to question the prosecution witnesses, but had no real idea of what to ask them. He simply kept repeating, at every chance he had, that he had not meant to kill the tavern keeper. This did him no good, however. The jury had little difficulty in coming to a verdict – they did not even bother to leave the box. John was found guilty, and a week later he was taken from Newgate Prison to Tyburn and there, along with a thief, a forger and another murderer, he was hanged. In the huge crowd which watched, there were many who were later to share his fate.

Later changes

In the hundred years which followed John's death, some changes were made for the better in the law. Prisoners were allowed to have lawyers to plead for them, and their witnesses were allowed to take the same oath as those for the prosecution. Something was done too about executions. The procession from Newgate to Tyburn was stopped, and criminals were now hanged just outside the prison – but still in public. On the other hand, the number of executions tended to increase, for Parliament was constantly adding to the number of crimes which carried the death penalty, until in 1776 223 people were hanged in London alone. What was more, although Howard and others like him did much to tell people what conditions in prisons were like, little was done to improve them until the nineteenth century.

Branding.

Punishments such as whipping were usually carried out in public outside the prison

Dates to remember

1665　The Plague of London
1666　The Fire of London

Things to do

1　Find out what would be done today if a case of plague were reported in a town. If there is a suitable local history, find out something about your own town or village in the seventeenth century. How big was the population? What sort of place was it? How did the people make their living? Were there any important trades? Was there a serious outbreak of the plague during the seventeenth century?

2　Try to find out where your local prison was in the seventeenth or eighteenth century. They often survive, as they were strongly built.

3　Try writing about some incident in your life as Evelyn and Pepys did in theirs.

Things to discuss

1　Read the following opinions on public executions. Which of them makes the stronger case? What other arguments could be brought forward on either side?

　　The first is written by Henry Fielding, a London magistrate.

> The design of those who first appointed executions to be public was to add the punishment of shame to that of death; in order to make the example an object of greater terror. But experience has shown us that the event is directly contrary to this intention. No good mind can avoid compassionating a set of wretches who are put to death we know not why, unless, as it almost appears, to make a holiday for, and to entertain, the mob.

On the other side was Dr Samuel Johnson. When it was suggested that it would be an improvement to stop public executions, he remarked:

> No, sir, it would not be an improvement. They object that the old method draws together a number of spectators. If they did not draw the spectators they would not answer their purpose. The old method is most satisfactory to all parties; the public is gratified with a procession; the criminal is supported by it. Why should all this be swept away?

2　Was Wren's plan for London really practicable?

Books to read

Selections from *Pepys Diary*
D. Defoe, *A Journal of the Plague Year*, Penguin
E. Murphy, *Samuel Pepys in London*, Longmans
M. Southwood, *John Howard*, Independent Press

Chapter 7
Colonies and wars 1603-1714

So far we have dealt mainly with what was going on in England itself. In this chapter we shall see how Englishmen were building up an overseas empire in the seventeenth century. In addition, we shall deal with the wars in which England became involved.

Early exploration

In the reign of Elizabeth, English sailors like Drake, Hawkins, and Raleigh had made many exciting voyages. In tiny frail ships, at the mercy of wind and weather, they had battled their way across the oceans of the world, landed in unknown countries and then struggled back, often ill and exhausted. They had not made such voyages for amusement – the risks were far too great for that – but for profit. A cargo of cloves from the East Indies could bring in a profit of 1000 per cent while one cargo of gold and silver from America might make a man rich for life. It was the lust for quick riches that sent Englishmen exploring, the hope that England, like Spain, might one day be at the

Empires in 1620. By 1610 the Dutch were also establishing an empire. (Map on page 96.)

Spanish

Portuguese

French

British

94

The Dutch trading post at Amboyna.

receiving end of a stream of gold and silver from across the sea. On the whole, they were disappointed.

Trading posts

In the seventeenth century, some of the glamour went out of exploration. Voyages across the oceans were now commonplace, and merchants in England were interested not so much in staking a lot on one voyage in the hope that it might make their fortunes, but rather in a steady return from a regular trade abroad. This meant that trading posts had to be established overseas, and this was done on a large scale. But England was not the only country interested in overseas trade. Spain already had a huge empire in South America, and Holland and France wanted to get their share as well. Unfortunately, the various countries did not make any attempt to share out the markets between them peacefully. They simply established their trading stations where they thought they could get most profit, and then fought off all comers. The result was that in the seventeenth and eighteenth centuries England became involved in wars with Holland, France and Spain over trade and overseas empire. In the end, thanks chiefly to her navy, England came out as the winner.

The East Indies

The Spice Islands of the East Indies formed one of the great centres of overseas trade in the sixteenth and seventeenth centuries.

The story of British trade in the area really begins in 1600, when Elizabeth I granted a charter to the East India Company, to trade with the East Indies. Armed with their charter, English merchants set out, only to discover that the Dutch had arrived there before them. None the less, they established a trading station at Amboyna. It was only a small post, with eighteen men, and their total armoury consisted of two muskets and three swords. It was not much, but it was enough to arouse

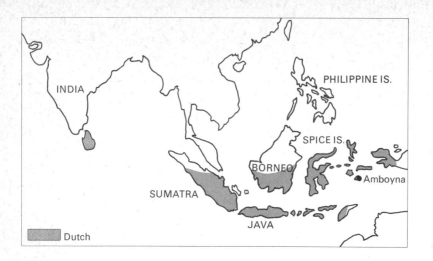

This map shows the hold that the Dutch had established over the East Indies. The British had little alternative to turning their attention to India itself.

the jealousy of the Dutch, who wanted to keep all the trade for themselves. In 1623 they captured a Japanese trader and tortured him until he 'confessed' that the English were planning to take over the Dutch fort at Amboyna, which was guarded by 600 well-armed soldiers. The story was clearly ridiculous, but it gave the Dutch the excuse they needed, and they captured and tortured the English traders until they too confessed. Ten of them were executed, and the post was abolished.

The Dutch Wars 1652–74

The 'Amboyna Massacre', as it was called, aroused great bitterness between England and Holland. Yet the Dutch still continued to carry huge quantities of English goods in their ships, which was very profitable. In 1651, as you read in Chapter 3, Parliament passed an act forbidding any foreign ship to carry English goods. The result was a succession of wars between England and Holland in the years between 1652 and 1674. These wars were fought mostly at sea. Blake was the greatest English admiral: Van Tromp the Dutch hero. Neither side really gained from the wars, and peace between the two countries was confirmed by the marriage of Charles II's niece, Mary, and the Dutch ruler, William of Orange.

War with Spain 1653–59

Meanwhile, Cromwell had also made war on Spain. The Spanish refused to allow Englishmen to trade with their American colonies, and Cromwell decided to teach them a lesson and extend the British Empire at the same time. He therefore sent an expedition to the West Indies and captured Jamaica, a Spanish possession. Later, in Europe, an English army, fighting side by side with the French, captured Dunkirk, which was part of the Spanish Netherlands. When peace was made in 1659 Dunkirk was handed over to England, but it was little real use, and Charles II's government sold it to France. (See Chapter 4.)

One of the Dutch tortures was, literally, to fill their victims with water.

Friends to foes

Charles II and James II continued the policy which Cromwell had begun by keeping on good terms with France, whose king, Louis XIV, was the richest and most powerful in Europe. But after 1689 this policy was reversed. It was to Louis that James had fled when the Revolution had driven him out of England, and Louis had welcomed him and recognized him as the rightful king of England. This annoyed the British government, but in any case England's new king, William III, and Louis were old enemies, for Louis had tried more than once to invade William's home country, Holland. This meant that England soon found herself at war with France. James himself (with French help) invaded Ireland in 1690, but was defeated. From then until 1713 England and France were constantly at war.

These wars were fought with great determination. William III, with the power of England behind him, saw his opportunity to put the

This Dutch print shows an English warship of the 1650s under sail.

French king in his place once and for all. He appointed as his ministers men from the Whig party who thought as he did, so that even when he died in 1702 and was succeeded by his sister-in-law, James's younger daughter Anne, the same policy was carried on. Anne, who was a very ordinary sort of woman, was usually prepared to follow the advice of her ministers on important matters.

The Duke of Marlborough

But more than ministers are needed to fight a war. Soldiers and generals are wanted as well. There was never a shortage of troops, but good generals are always rare and William and Anne were fortunate in that they had John Churchill, Duke of Marlborough, to serve them. Marlborough seemed at first sight to be just a middle-aged courtier and was, indeed, quite at home at formal receptions and conferences. Dressed in the height of fashion, smiling and pleasant to all, never losing his temper, he looked far more suited to making peace treaties than to fighting battles. He always kept on good terms with anyone he thought might be useful to him and, when he went on a campaign, he always left his wife at court to maintain his influence with the Queen. As Queen Anne was easily led, and the Duchess of Marlborough was very strong-willed and resolute, this worked quite well, and the power of the Marlboroughs and their Whig friends seemed supreme and settled.

This engraving shows the violence and confusion of a sea battle of this period. Often ships were completely hidden in the smoke from their own cannons. Here boarding parties are being sent out.

Yet however good a courtier, Marlborough's real genius was as a general. He had helped to crush the Monmouth rebellion in 1685, and had fought in other campaigns since, but was not given supreme command of the British forces until 1702 because William suspected, quite rightly, that the Duke was still keeping in touch with the exiled James II. Once in command, Marlborough was superb. He showed himself to be brave and resolute, so that his men came to admire him. His charm and patience enabled him to get on well with allied generals when others would have found it impossible, while his quick and daring mind could plan campaigns and battles in such an original way that the enemy were always taken by surprise. Not one detail would be overlooked. To give some idea of how Marlborough worked here is an account of one of his campaigns – perhaps his greatest, that of 1704.

The crisis of 1704

In the spring of 1704 the English and their allies were in a very weak position. Part of Holland was occupied by one French army, and Vienna was threatened by another. It looked as though the alliance of Holland, Austria and England against France would be knocked to pieces and Louis XIV would emerge victorious after all. But Marlborough had thought of a daring plan which, if it worked, would completely turn the tables on the French. He proposed simply to march an army of 40,000 men from Holland right across Germany to the Danube, a

A portrait of Marlborough painted by Sir Godfrey Kneller.

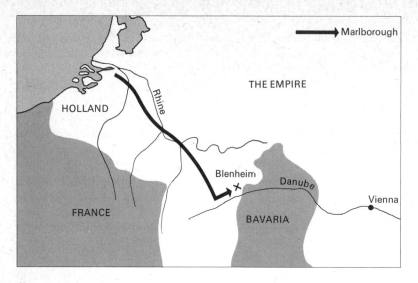

The route followed by Marlborough across Europe.

By the end of the seventeenth century all infantrymen were armed with muskets. The invention of the bayonet enabled them to be used in the same way as pikes when the occasion demanded.

distance of some 400 miles, join with Prince Eugene, the Austrian general, and then deliver the French and their German allies such a blow that they would not be able to fight in that part of Europe again.

The Great March

There were all sorts of dangers and drawbacks in such a plan. In the first place, Marlborough had to persuade the Dutch to allow him to take some of their troops away from defending Holland. He did not tell them how far he intended to take them, and in the end he got permission to lead an expedition down the Rhine. He knew that once he was gone, they could do nothing to bring him back. Not that the Dutch were the only people to be kept in ignorance of Marlborough's plans. It was essential that the French should not guess where he was taking his army until it was too late for them to do anything to counter the move. He therefore kept the whole scheme secret, even from his wife, and when the army moved off in May, nobody had the slightest idea that he intended marching right into Austria.

So far, then, all was well, but there were still many difficulties ahead. The task of moving 40,000 men with cavalry and artillery across 400 miles of strange and, in some cases, enemy country, along eighteenth-century roads was no small one. As a rule, such marches caused almost as many casualties as a battle, and the troops reached their destination exhausted and footsore, in no condition to fight a campaign. What was more, it was common for them to live off the country as they passed through, so that they left a trail of poverty and hatred behind them, thus turning allies into enemies.

Now Marlborough was determined to fall into none of these traps. Everything was organized; nothing left to chance. At dawn each day the troops broke camp and marched off. If they came to a river, they found a bridge of boats prepared for them, and so were able to cross without any loss of time. Long before noon they had covered twelve or fifteen miles and reached their next stopping place, where they found that food was already being prepared for them. 'The soldiers', wrote one officer, 'had nothing to do but pitch their tents, boil their kettles and lie down to rest.' The food which they ate had been paid for in cash so that the army was popular with local farmers. Any soldiers who fell ill were properly cared for and new shoes were even available for those who had worn out their first pair. Experienced soldiers had seen nothing like it in years of campaigning and were full of praise for their general, through whose efforts alone all this was possible. As a result when, on 11 June, Prince Eugene greeted Marlborough's troops, he was 'very surprised to find them in so good a condition after so long a march', speaking admiringly of the lively air of each and every one of them. Indeed, they were probably fitter at the end of their march than they had been at the beginning, and by the end of June they had reached the Danube, ready to give battle.

Blenheim

The French army in Austria, under the command of Marshal Tallard, was very large. In addition, it was drawn up in a very strong position, centred on the little village of Blenheim. To the south was the broad sweep of the Danube, while to the north lay an area of marshy ground crossed by streams which emptied into the river. Farther north lay forested mountains. Blenheim itself was strongly fortified, and surely no commander would be so mad as to send an army into the attack across a swamp, or over mountain slopes! Tallard felt quite safe. Even when he heard that the allied army was approaching, the Frenchman could not believe that an attack was intended, and sent troops out into the country as usual to bring in supplies.

The battle

But Tallard was wrong. Marlborough knew that to achieve anything worthwhile, he had to attack and defeat the French army at whatever cost. Accordingly, on the morning of 13 August 1704, the allied army advanced slowly along the river bank towards the village of Blenheim. By 9 a.m. the troops were drawn up facing the French positions, and the French were able to bombard them with cannon shot. Soon they got their range and were causing heavy casualties among Marlborough's men. But he had to wait until noon, for Prince Eugene had not yet got all his troops in position. Finally, all was ready, and the allied troops launched a furious attack on the village itself. The leader of the attack, Brigadier Rowe, forbade his troops to fire until they reached the actual defences of the village. Indeed, he finally gave the signal by sticking his sword into the woodwork of the first barricades. He and many of his men were killed in this attack, but its ferocity so frightened the French that they hastily took men from the centre and crammed them into the village to repel any further assaults.

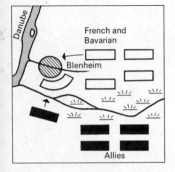

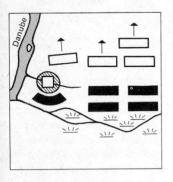

Diagram of the Battle of Blenheim, 1704.

The breakthrough

This left the centre weakly defended and was just what Marlborough
wanted. Slowly his infantry advanced across the marshy ground,
picking their way carefully, using planks and bundles of brushwood
to cross the worst patches. Under fire all the way, they finally reached
the other side and then opened fire with their muskets to cover the
cavalry who crossed on foot, leading their horses by the bridle. Once
across, they mounted, and were ready for battle. They needed to be,
for the French attacked them again and again, trying to drive them
back. But all was in vain, for more and more troops poured across.
At about five o'clock, Marlborough ordered them to charge. For a
moment, the white-coated Frenchmen, although tired and dispirited,
seemed to stand their ground. Then the fast-trotting cavalry swept
them away, and fanned out to pursue them. Many, including Tallard,
were captured. Others tried to swim the Danube and were drowned.

This engraving shows the
crucial point of the battle. The
river Danube flows across the
left of the scene. Marlborough's
troops have just broken through
in the centre and are driving
towards the river to cut off the
French troops trapped in the
village. Marshal Tallard is
already a prisoner in
Marlborough's coach.

Within a short time the French troops in Blenheim itself, surrounded on all sides, surrendered too. Marlborough's victory was complete. Fumbling in his pocket he found a tavern bill, and on the back of it he wrote to his wife as follows:

Aug. 13 1704

I have not time to say more, but to beg you will give my duty to the Queen, and let her know her army has had a Glorious Victory. Monsieur Tallard and two other generals are in my coach and I am following the rest: the bearer my Aide de Camp, Col Parke, will give her an account of what has passed. I shall do it in a day or two by another more at large.

Marlborough

Marlborough's fall

News of Marlborough's great victory at Blenheim soon spread all over

103

Europe and gave fresh heart to England's allies. He was the hero of the hour and in England the Whig politicians used his success to make themselves more popular. In the years that followed, Marlborough won three more victories which brought France to her knees, but Louis XIV refused to make peace because the English government offered him such bad terms. As the war dragged on, the Tories accused Marlborough and his friends of fighting on just to get more glory for themselves, and they eventually persuaded Queen Anne to dismiss the Duke and appoint some Tory ministers who at once made peace with France by the Treaty of Utrecht. But Anne did not really trust them, and soon brought the Whigs back again. None the less, it was the end of Marlborough. For a time he lived abroad, but spent the last years of his life at his great house, Blenheim Palace, in Oxfordshire.

The Scots and the succession

One great problem in Anne's reign was the succession to the throne. Although Anne was pregnant at least seventeen times, she only had six children, all of whom died when young. This meant that she had no direct heir, and the English Parliament decided that when she died, the throne should go to her German cousins who ruled the little state of Hanover. This irritated the Scots, who had not been consulted, and when the English Parliament declared who should succeed Anne as the ruler of England, the Scottish Parliament promptly retorted that when the time came, they would choose their own king for Scotland. This alarmed the English government. They felt sure that the Scots would choose James II's son, James, who was a Catholic, living in France. Then England would be trapped between the French in the south and the Scots in the north. At all costs this had to be prevented, and in 1707 the English found a way to make sure that it could never happen. This was simply to combine England and Scotland into one Kingdom. Since 1603, when James I had become King of England, the two countries had been ruled by the same king, but Scotland had still kept its own Parliament, Council and system of law. Now it was proposed to unite the two kingdoms into one and abolish the Scottish Parliament. In 1707 the two Parliaments passed the necessary acts and the Scottish Parliament ceased to exist. Instead there were 45 Scottish members in the new United Kingdom Parliament at Westminster.

George I comes to the throne

In 1714, Queen Anne died, and the throne passed to her German cousin, George of Hanover. He had never been to England in his life and hated the thought of coming. He could not speak English well, and took no interest in English people or English politics. His accession to the throne was not popular in England. Nobody really liked him, but most English people were prepared to put up with him. After all, the only alternative to him was the Catholic, James. If he became King, he might try to bring back the Catholic religion and ally England with France. Cer-

No copper coins were struck in Anne's reign until 1714. By the time this farthing was ready for circulation, Anne was dead.

tainly all the Whigs thought that however unpleasant George might be, he was less dangerous than James. Only a few Tories, called Jacobites, thought that James had the better right, and used to drink toasts to the King over the water.

Such was the demand that halfpennies were struck in nine years of George I's reign.

Dates to remember

1600	Foundation of East India Company
1623	Massacre of Amboyna
1674	End of Dutch Wars
1704	Battle of Blenheim
1707	Act of Union
1714	Death of Queen Anne

Things to do

1 Find out ways in which Scottish law is still different from English law.
2 Find out more about Marlborough's other campaigns.

Books to read

M. C. Borer, *Famous Rogues* (Chapter on Sir Henry Morgan), Longmans
J. L. Davies (ed.), *The Mayflower and the Pilgrim Fathers*, Cape (Jackdaw)
E. Garnett, *Queen Anne and Her Times*, Black
D. Johnson (ed.), *Marlborough*, Cape (Jackdaw)
R. J. Mitchell, *A Country Doctor in the Days of Queen Anne*, Longmans
N. Wymer, *Soldiers and Sailors* (Chapter on Marlborough), Oxford University Press

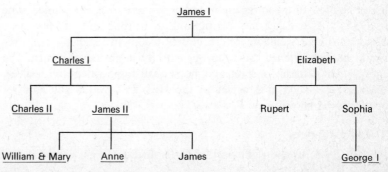

George I's position in the English royal family.

Chapter 8
Politics, rebellions and colonies 1714-45

The Fifteen

As we pointed out in the last chapter, the vast majority of Englishmen accepted George I and his descendants as their Kings. In the Scottish Highlands, however, there were many who were prepared to strike a blow in favour of James Stuart. In 1715 a rebellion broke out there. It was badly organized. The Marquess of Ormonde was to have led a rising in England at the same time, but it never materialized. What was more, James himself never really believed that the rising had any chance of success. He was rather a gloomy young man, with little drive or enthusiasm. He only consented to have any part in the business because Louis XIV promised to help, but, just before the rebellion broke out, Louis died, leaving the throne to his great-grandson, who was only a child. France was ruled by a regent who was anxious to keep on friendly terms with the English. He therefore refused to help James, who promptly lost all enthusiasm. When the Scots proclaimed him king, he was still in France and did not reach Scotland until the rebellion was as good as over. He returned wearily to France to continue his comfortable exile. The Stuart peril seemed to be over.

Bonny Prince Charlie

Thirty years went by. James married, had two sons, and passed into middle age. England, under George I and his son, prospered. Less and less was heard of the Jacobites, and but for one man the Stuart kings across the water might have been forgotten altogether. This was Charles Edward, James's elder son. A complete contrast to his father, Charles was quick and decisive, bold and enthusiastic – a man of action. He had, moreover, the gift of infecting other people with his enthusiasm. He could make the impossible seem easy. To him it was unbearable that the rightful King of England should be content to spend his life in exile in a foreign country and he resolved at the first opportunity to strike at least one blow to try to regain his father's inheritance. His chance came in 1745. The British army was fighting in Europe and had just been defeated. There would therefore be few troops in England, and they would be disheartened. Such an opportunity might never return. The French lent Charles a ship, and he set sail for Scotland with a few friends. He landed at Moidart in the Highlands on 23 July and set about raising an army.

The Highlanders

He had come to the right part of Great Britain to get soldiers. The

Portrait of a clan chief, Lord George Murray, carrying his sword and shield. His dirk is at his belt.

Highlands of Scotland were inhabited by the clansmen, who were a race apart. They spoke Gaelic, and lived a hard life as herdsmen. They were used to fighting to protect their herds, and were violent and headstrong. They were entirely ruled by their clan chiefs, who had the power of life and death over them, and owned all the land occupied by the clan. All the members of the clan had the same surname as their chief, and thought it their duty to protect him and the good name of the clan. Their chief weapons were swords and daggers, which they called claymores and dirks, and in battle they carried round leather shields. They were formidable fighters, for they charged with such ferocity, yelling and shouting like maniacs, that they struck fear into the very hearts of their foes. Indeed, their appearance alone was frightening. They were ragged and unkempt and their only clothing was a length of tartan cloth, part of which was wrapped round the waist to form a sort of skirt, and the rest passed round the chest, over one shoulder, and was secured by a bodkin. The chief of the clan was better dressed. He wore tartan trousers, jacket and waistcoat, and had a tartan cloak. In his bonnet he wore an eagle feather to mark his rank, and he carried pistols, dirk and sword. He was a formidable figure. It was estimated that he and his fellow-chiefs could call on the services of over 30,000 Highlanders.

The Forty-five

It was to such men as these that young Charles Edward appealed for help to win the throne of England for his father. He did not ask in vain. There was something about his courage and daring that they could not resist and soon Charles was able to set out for the Lowlands with an army of well over 5,000 at his back. He defeated a royal army, and entered Edinburgh in triumph. He held a great reception at Holyrood Palace, and Scotland seemed to be his. But this was only a part of his father's inheritance. There was still England to conquer. So, with his faithful Highlanders behind him, Charles entered England and marched south, hoping to gather supporters as he went. He failed to do so. The English gazed curiously and rather fearfully at the young prince and his strange army, so oddly dressed and speaking one to another in a queer foreign tongue. They were pleased and surprised that the Highlanders did not lay waste the countryside, and were amazed at the discipline of the force, but they made no attempt to join it. They would have felt ill at ease in such company and, in any case, they were prosperous and contented. Thus Charles's men marched on, farther and farther from their Highland homes, deeper and deeper into a foreign country.

Meanwhile in London all was panic and confusion. The Bank of England, established by William III, was besieged by people drawing out their money, and the courtiers were preparing to leave for Hanover. They need not have worried, for as the Scotsmen moved closer to London, their spirits sank lower and lower. There were still only 5,000

Charles Edward in full highland dress.

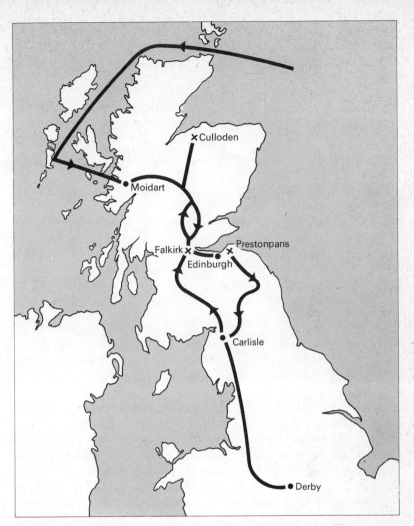

The thick line shows the route taken by Charles Edward. The names of the principal battles are also given.

of them, and they were liable to be cut off from their homes by the troops who were being brought back from abroad to crush the rebellion. Murmurings and grumblings steadily increased, and when the Scottish forces reached Derby in December 1745, the clan leaders approached Charles and told him they wished to go back to Scotland. Charles was horrified. He felt it was throwing away a wonderful chance. He pleaded with them to change their minds, but they were determined and he could not shake them. 'I will go on', he is said to have cried in despair, 'while one of you will come with me.' None of them offered to do so. The next day the army turned north, and began to retrace its footsteps towards Scotland.

Culloden

As the Scots went north, the government gathered their army and sent it after them. This army was commanded by young William, Duke of

109

Cumberland, George II's son. He was only twenty-five, but was quite an experienced commander, with a reputation for hardness and severity. He pressed on into Scotland, and on 16 April 1746 he met Charles and the rebel army on Culloden Moor, just outside Inverness. The Scots charged with great courage, but Cumberland's men drove them back and scattered them. Many of the clansmen died in the battle, and those who lay wounded were afterwards killed by Cumberland's men. Charles himself rode from the field, and after being hunted around Scotland for five months, finally took ship for France. Exile did not suit him, and he took to drink, so that when he died in 1788 he was a pathetic, drunken old man, a sad contrast to the young prince who had inspired the clansmen forty-three years before.

This engraving of the Battle of Culloden was not published until 1797. A Highland attack is driven off *(right)* while the royal troops *(left)* attack the rebel flank through a gap in a wall. It is probably more imaginative than accurate.

The pacification of the Highlands

Culloden was more than the end of Charles's hopes of winning the English throne. It was also the end of the clan system. All the land of the clans which had taken part in the rebellion was plundered and many innocent clansmen were murdered. Meanwhile the leaders of the rising were tried and executed. But this was not all. To make quite sure that the Highlands would not give trouble again, Parliament passed a law taking all power from the clan chiefs and another forbidding the wearing of the kilt or any sort of clan tartan. What was more, all fire-arms in the Highlands were confiscated. These acts were enforced with great severity, and the clans were broken. When, in 1782, they once again permitted them to wear their tartan, few bothered to do so. It was not until George IV appeared in Edinburgh in a kilt that the Highland dress became popular once again.

Robert Walpole

One of the reasons for the lack of support for Charles in England was the work done by Robert Walpole, who was in charge of the country's government for twenty-one years. Now, to remain in power for so long, Walpole had to be a very clever politician, but he did not give that impression. He was short and stout, with a round, plain commonsense sort of face. There was no sort of dignity about his looks or his manners. He seemed to be an ordinary down-to-earth countryman, who would have been at home on a farm, or in a country town on market day. It was difficult to imagine him presiding over a meeting of ministers or addressing the House of Commons. Yet he was the King's chief minister for longer than anyone else before or since. How did he do it?

To begin with, he was very much more intelligent than he looked, and, in particular, he understood finances much better than any other politician of his day. Almost the first thing he did when he came to power was to see the country through a dangerous financial crisis and he was later able to introduce many reforms which helped England to become one of the most prosperous countries in the world. So long as the country was getting richer, Walpole could be sure of the support of those merchants and traders who were benefiting from it, and they had a good deal of influence.

Walpole as Prime Minister.

Walpole and the Commons

Next, Walpole understood human nature, and this enabled him to get on well with the House of Commons and with the King. So far as the House of Commons was concerned, he knew that most of its members would not vote for the government regularly unless they were given some sort of reward. 'All these men have their price,' he said, and he gave those members who supported his government well-paid posts, many of which had little or no work attached to them. The members knew perfectly well that they had only to vote against Walpole to lose these posts, and therefore supported him whenever they could. If he found that any of his ideas were so unpopular that M.P.s were prepared to vote against it in spite of his bribes, then he would not try to force it through. Instead, he simply abandoned it. In this way he usually got on well with the House of Commons.

Walpole and the King

As for the King, Walpole realized that George I was only too pleased to be able to hand over all the routine work of government to someone he could trust. George could not, in any case, have presided over meetings of ministers as William and Anne had done, for he spoke little

English. Walpole took over from him, taking reports of the meetings back to the King, with whom he conversed in Latin. George liked Walpole's shrewdness and commonsense, and trusted him completely. Even after George's death in 1727, his son George II, and Queen Caroline, gave Walpole their support too, for there was nobody who could do the job better. This made some people jealous. Walpole, they said, was not just an ordinary minister. He was first among the ministers – a Prime Minister. Sir Robert protested, but the title stuck, and the work taken over by Walpole from the King has been done by the Prime Minister ever since.

Eighteenth-century elections

The support of the King was particularly important at election times. Eighteenth-century elections were very different from today's. We take it for granted that everybody over twenty-one has the vote and that the voting is done in secret, which means that it is impossible to bribe or compel any elector to vote for any particular candidate. In the eighteenth

An election entertainment. The voters are encouraged to eat – and drink – their fill at the candidate's expense. The rival party throw bricks and stones in through the window, and their ardour is cooled by water being poured over them. An injured man has his cut head bathed in gin *(foreground)*.

century only a very few men had the vote, and they had to go and declare them in public when the election was held. This meant that it was easy to bribe or threaten electors to make them vote the way you wanted. It was accepted that votes could be bought and sold and, when both Whigs and Tories were bidding for them, their price might well reach £100 each. This made elections very expensive and, as a result, the government decided in future that they should take place every seven instead of every three years. The King had a good deal of influence over elections. Indeed, he controlled many seats completely and Walpole could be certain that whoever was elected by such places would be sure to support him.

The Empire: India

Thus, with the support of the King, Parliament and the people, Walpole seemed secure for ever. What was more, trade was increasing and the Empire was growing. After the Massacre of Amboyna, the East India Company turned their attention to the mainland of India and had

Here the votes are polled. The contest must be close, as a cripple with one leg is being polled, together with a madman. Behind them in the queue are a prisoner, still in his irons, a dying man carried by his friends, and a blind man.

established trading posts there. For instance, Charles II gave them Bombay, which he had been granted by the Portuguese as part of his wife's dowry. Trade expanded, profits were high and in 1696 the Company established another post at Calcutta, which soon became the most prosperous of all. From 1700 until 1740 the directors of the Company in London sat back and watched the money roll in as the bales of cotton and spices were unloaded at London and Bristol, and the great ships swung majestically back out to sea to fetch more. This was what the directors liked: regular voyages and regular profits.

The East India Wharf near London Bridge, with a selection of the cargoes brought from India in the East Indiamen, as the company's ships were called.

America

In America, too, Britain had important possessions. These had been developing all through the seventeenth century. The first English settlement there had been made in Virginia in the reign of Elizabeth I. It had not survived, but in 1607 another party went out. Thanks mainly to the

A contemporary engraving of John Smith.

work of John Smith, a brave and determined man, they were able to get on reasonable terms with the local Indians who naturally objected to people settling on grounds over which they had hunted for hundreds of years. Soon the settlers were growing and selling tobacco, and were quite prosperous. As they became stronger, they were less frightened of the Indians, and did not bother to keep on good terms with them any longer. The result was a dreadful massacre in 1622, in which many settlers were killed. In revenge the settlers killed thousands of Indians, but from then on they were careful to treat the Indians with greater consideration, while the Indians now thought twice before attacking white settlers. Thus for many years the two races lived at peace, even though the Virginians were steadily taking more and more land from the Indian hunting grounds.

The labour problem

One of the biggest problems facing the settlers was that of a labour supply. Clearly nobody was going to leave Britain and voyage for weeks across a stormy and dangerous ocean just to become a labourer on a plantation. They could be farm labourers at home. They went to America to own land of their own, and make money. Yet somebody had to do the work on the land. The Indians were no good; they were hunters and did not want to settle and work on the land for somebody else. The only answer was to import labourers from other countries. First, convicts were shipped over from England to cultivate the cotton and tobacco plantations, but they were not used to the climate, and died off quickly. In any case, there were not enough of them. The real answer to the problem was found when an enterprising merchant landed in West Africa, bought some prisoners from a native chief, shipped them across the Atlantic, and sold them to the plantation owners on the other side to use as slaves. Details of this trade are given in *A History of Britain* volume 4.

As a result of it the colonists in the south grew rich, built themselves comfortable mansions, and lived a leisured gentleman's life. Soon there were several other colonies besides Virginia depending on slavery for their prosperity.

The Northern colonies

Farther north the story was very different. The first settlers there went, not to make money, but to found a Puritan community. These were the famous Pilgrim Fathers, who sailed from England in 1620 to escape from James I's persecution and founded New England. There the atmosphere was not at all like that in the south. The colonists were stern, hard-working men, whose religion was all-important to them. What was more, the climate was not suited to growing tobacco and cotton, and the settlers lived by farming and fishing. Laud's activities in England encouraged many more Puritans to come over, and, later, Quakers too came to found a colony in

This print shows the popular idea of what an Indian looked like.

115

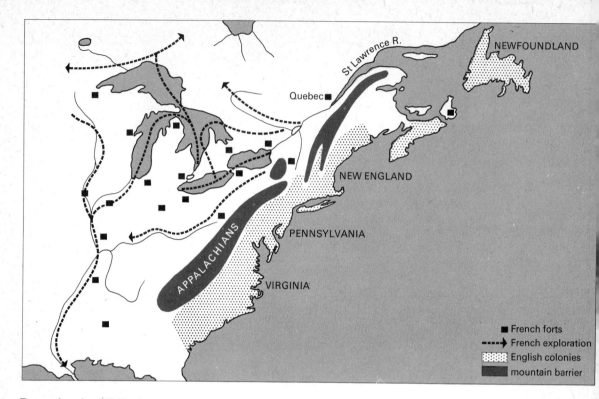

Pennsylvania. While the southerners tended to live like country gentlemen, the northerners were more industrious and down-to-earth. They, too, progressed.

English and French possessions in North America, at the beginning of the eighteenth century.

Captain Jenkins

Thus by 1738 England had a considerable empire with which to trade. There were thirteen colonies stretched down the east coast of America, and many trading posts in India. But even this was not enough. Some British adventurers wanted to trade with other countries' colonies as well. One, Captain Jenkins, insisted on carrying on an illegal trade with Spain's colonies. As a result, his ship was boarded and searched and Jenkins claimed that his ear was cut off in the resulting struggle. He came back to England, with his ear in a box, demanding war with Spain.

Walpole and war

Walpole had no sympathy with Jenkins. He had no use for glory, and hated war. It seemed to him to be a waste of money and life, and he was quite prepared to let other countries fight each other while Britain remained at peace and made money. 'There are 50,000 men slain this year in Europe,' he told the Queen proudly in 1734, 'and not one Englishman.' Now many of his fellow-countrymen did not agree with his attitude. After twenty years of peace, they were quite prepared to risk the wealth of the country in taking on the French or the Spanish, and they disliked the way in which Walpole went out of his way to avoid war. Thus, when Jenkins told his story, there was a great storm of protest and Walpole, much against his will, was forced to declare war on Spain. 'They now ring their bells,' he remarked bitterly as he listened to the bells ringing out in triumph and excitement, 'but they will soon wring their hands.'

Sir Robert was right. He was no good at waging war and it did not go well. In 1742, he resigned and retired to the House of Lords as Earl of Orford. For the next twenty years Britain was at war, first with Spain and then with France. But Walpole was not the only politician who was not a success as a war leader. Those who replaced him were no better, and, as the wars dragged on and Britain seemed to be gaining nothing from them, the complaints grew louder and louder. After all, what proof was there that these politicians were really doing their best? Everybody knew that they were elected through bribery, and kept themselves in office by the same means. Such men, it was argued, cared only for money, and loved their own welfare and comfort more than they did their country. What was needed was a leader who was honest and efficient and, above all, one who could be trusted to put the welfare of his country above all else.

The reverse of seventeenth and eighteenth century copper coins bore the figure of Britannia. This George II halfpenny is larger than today's.

Dates to remember

1715   First Jacobite Rebellion
1721   Walpole became Prime Minister
1738   Captain Jenkins complained to the Commons
1742   Walpole resigned
1745   Second Jacobite rebellion

Things to do

1   Find a song about Charles Edward.
2   Find out more about John Smith.
3   Find out which towns in your own county elected Members of Parliament in the eighteenth century.
4   Many American towns were named after British counterparts. Using an atlas, find out whether there are any towns in your part of the country which have American namesakes. If so, find out what you can about the history of the American towns concerned.

Books to read

J. L. Davies (ed.), *The Fifteen and the Forty-Five*, Cape (Jackdaw)
W. J. C. Gill, *Captain John Smith and Virginia*, Longmans
F. Grice, *Rebels and Fugitives* (Chapters on Bonnie Prince Charlie and the Earl of Derwentwater), Batsford
L. F. James, *A Settler in New England*, Oxford University Press
P. Rush, *Strange Stuarts* (Chapter on John Smith), Hutchinson
W. Stevenson, *The Jacobite Rising of 1745*, Longmans

Chapter 9
The age of Pitt

Pitt the man

There was, fortunately, one politician who had the ability to lead his country in a crisis. His name was William Pitt. Born in 1708, Pitt entered Parliament in 1735 as an opponent of Walpole. He was honest and fearless and soon showed himself to be a powerful orator, drenching Walpole and his ministers in a shower of scorn. He refused all offers of bribes, and soon became very popular with the people. Yet it was not until 1757, when England seemed to be losing the war against France, that he was put in charge of affairs. This was because his fellow-politicians did not like him, which is easy to understand. For one thing, they objected to the way that Pitt pretended to be better than they were just because he did not take bribes. What was more, he was very conceited and impatient. This made him very difficult to work with, for he was always convinced that his ideas were right, and would not listen to the opinions of others. As he grew older, his conceit passed all bounds, and several times toppled him into madness. Yet only Pitt could provide the decisive leadership the country needed in a war.

The Seven Years War   1756–63

The situation which confronted Pitt in 1757 was desperate. Britain had fought European wars before, but now she was confronted with a struggle in Europe, America and India simultaneously, and this struggle lasted for seven years. British settlers and traders in India and America had clashed with Frenchmen who had also settled there and were now seeking to establish their superiority.

Duquesne in America

In America, the French possessions stretched from Canada in the north to the Mississippi in the south. Here the French, under Duquesne, built a series of forts to defend their frontier. The British colonists claimed that one of these forts was built on Virginian territory, and in 1755 a British force was sent to capture it, but was completely crushed. This was only the beginning, and for two years the French had such a number of successes that it began to look as if the English might be driven into the sea. It was not a good outlook for Pitt.

Dupleix in India

In India, the situation was less critical, though it had been very serious a few years earlier. Here, too, the French had a capable and ambitious governor, named Dupleix, who had taken charge of the French trading

Cartoon of Pitt in old age. He suffered so badly from gout that he could not move without crutches.

The House of Commons in 1741. The layout is still the same as in 1624, but the benches now have backs, and galleries have been provided.

post of Pondicherry in 1741. He was determined to expand French trade and to drive the British out of India. He thought that by making alliances with the Indian princes he could get such a large army together that he would be able to crush the tiny English forces. He almost succeeded. In 1746 he captured and destroyed Madras, and paraded its governor through the streets of Pondicherry. The French government ordered him to hand Madras back to the English, but Dupleix had shown his strength, and all India seemed at his mercy.

Robert Clive

Among those who had to flee from Madras when it was captured by the French was a young clerk named Robert Clive. He was intelligent and proud, and was so angry at the French success, that he asked to be transferred to the Company's army. His request was granted and he showed such coolness and courage in his new job that he was put in

119

command of 500 men – all that the Company could spare – to launch an attack on Arcot, the capital city of one of the princes allied to the French. To the amazement of all, Clive not only captured the city, but held its castle against 10,000 attackers, in spite of the fact that his soldiers were starving. He became famous overnight, especially among the Indians, who called him 'Subit Jang', or 'Resolute in War'. They would fight anywhere under his command.

This was just as well, for there was plenty of fighting to be done. Dupleix was recalled by the French government, but his Indian allies still had to be dealt with. For instance, in 1756 the ruler of Bengal captured Calcutta and, according to one story, imprisoned 146 British prisoners in a room eighteen feet by twenty-five feet, with the result that 123 of them died of suffocation. It is by no means certain that this did in fact take place, but it was widely believed, and Clive launched an immediate attack on Bengal. He defeated its ruler at the battle of Plassey, and put another in his place. Thus, through Clive's initiative, India at least was safe in 1757. America was the weakest point.

Pitt's policy

Once Pitt took charge, he set to work to snatch victory from defeat. For the first time he fought the war on a planned basis all over the world. His idea was to use British naval strength to maintain and supply armies in America and India to capture French colonies there, while he paid the King of Prussia to fight against French troops in Europe. He had no use for the ordinary rules of promotion in the services and appointed lively young men with ideas to command armies.

He realized the importance of the war in America and sent some of his best men over there, with the necessary ships and men. Gradually through 1758 and 1759 the French were driven back and in the autumn of 1759 came the capture of the great French stronghold of Quebec.

Wolfe at Quebec

This was achieved by General Wolfe, perhaps the greatest of Pitt's generals. He tried in vain to attack Quebec from the front, and to bombard it. His men were falling ill, and winter was fast approaching. Then, at his wits' end, he heard of a narrow path leading up from the river to the heights above the town. On the night of 12 September, boats carried the troops quietly downstream under the very eyes of the enemy and put them ashore at the foot of the path. By the time that dawn broke, the army was drawn up ready to attack. The French came out to meet it and were defeated. Wolfe was killed, and so was the French commander, Montcalm. But Quebec was captured, and by the end of 1760 all the French in North America had surrendered.

Pitt's resignation and the Peace of Paris

By 1761, France was having the worst of the war and Pitt could see a

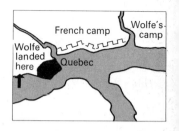

Quebec on the St Lawrence river. Just before the battle, Wolfe moved his camp upstream, to the left of the arrow.

An English engraving showing how Wolfe's troops were landed on the river bank near Quebec. The scale is rather odd, the boats being much too large and the river bank not nearly high enough.

chance of giving Britain complete trade supremacy. With France at bay, he favoured an attack on Spain so that her colonies, too, could be captured. The other members of the government would not agree and Pitt, furious and resentful, resigned. The war dragged on for two more years and then in 1763 the Treaty of Paris was signed. Canada was handed over to Britain, together with some trading posts in India. On the other hand, French sugar islands in the West Indies, captured as a result of England's naval supremacy, were handed back, and France was given fishing rights off the North American coast.

When the terms of the treaty became known, Pitt was beside himself with rage. Although ill and exhausted, he dragged himself to the House of Commons and denounced the treaty. He was afraid that France would rebuild her resources, wrest naval supremacy from Britain and recover her losses. England, he thought, should have smashed France for ever. 'We retain nothing', he cried, 'though we have conquered everything.'

121

A French engraving of the firework display organized in London to celebrate the Peace of Paris in 1763.

Although Pitt's views were popular with many merchants, he could not persuade the Commons, and the treaty was agreed in spite of his opposition.

India after 1763

After the Peace of Paris, the East India Company was left in complete control of an enormous area of India, and, as a result, profits rose. Yet so much power had its disadvantages too, for the Company found itself deeply involved in Indian politics. Now the men who were sent to India were merchants and clerks, not statesmen. They could deal with cargoes and ledgers, but were quite out of their depth when it came to politics. The Indian princes were, moreover, men of great wealth, willing to pay to get their way. The result was that the Company officials found themselves exposed to temptations which were, as Clive said, 'such as flesh and blood could not be expected to withstand'. In short, bribes were offered and accepted, the administration was inefficient and dishonest and the Company servants grew rich. The Governor of Bengal, a Company servant, with an income of £4,000,000 a year and an army of 30,000, ruled 26,000,000 subjects. In 1770 there was a dreadful famine in Bengal, and the poverty of the people there seemed so great a contrast to the wealth of the Company that the government decided that some power would have to be taken from the Company.

In fact, two acts were passed, which left the Company free to trade, but brought the government of the country under the control of the British Government. In the meantime, Warren Hastings was sent out to Bengal, and he reformed the government and administration there. So suspicious were some politicians of all those who had ruled in India that even he was accused of dishonesty and oppression, and was only found not guilty after a trial lasting seven years. Still, he did not suffer in vain, for however ambitious and intolerant future British officials in India were, they were usually honest and efficient.

A British trading station, probably Madras. The engraver has done his best to include as many typically Indian things as possible.

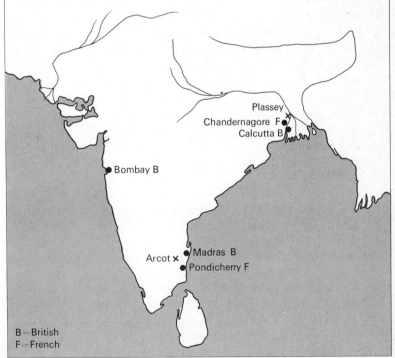

The main British and French possessions in India. (Calcutta is the capital of Bengal province.)

B = British
F = French

123

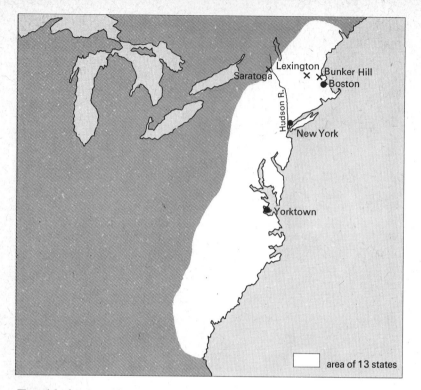

area of 13 states

The thirteen colonies, with the sites of the main battles.

Trouble in America

The difficulties in India were nothing compared to the disaster which struck Britain in America, where relations between the British government and the colonies grew worse and worse, until in 1775, war broke out between them. The trouble started almost as soon as the French had been defeated, for even though the war was over, the British government decided that it was necessary to keep a British army in North America, in case the French tried to recapture what they had lost. This army would be very expensive, and it was thought only fair that the colonists should pay their share towards its upkeep. This could be done by levying fresh taxes in America, and making sure that the Navigation Acts were properly enforced. As it was, they were being ignored for most of the time, and the Americans were trading with whom they pleased. Once having made up their minds, the British government made all the necessary arrangements and waited for the money to come in.

The result was a storm of protest, which amazed and upset them. The Americans did not think that the British Parliament ought to have any power over them. They had their own assemblies where people whom they had elected, discussed and voted those taxes which they had to pay. They had no vote or voice in the British Parliament. Why, then, should they pay taxes just because the British Parliament asked them to? They refused to pay a penny. What was more, they were amazed at the attempt to enforce the Navigation Acts. They only put up with these acts because nobody ever really took them seriously. The idea of trading only with Britain seemed so stupid that they decided to resist the British government's demands.

The War of American Independence

The colonists were not alone in thinking that the English government was being unreasonable. Pitt, who had done so much to win the war against the French in North America, agreed with them. He said he rejoiced that the colonists had resisted, and urged the government to cancel their demands. But the government was afraid to appear weak, and although they removed some of the taxes, they left others, just to show that they had the right to impose them if they liked. Gradually the position grew worse and there were a number of incidents. In 1770 a number of colonists in Boston were killed when they threw snowballs at some soldiers, and the soldiers fired back. In 1772 a coastguard ship was captured and burned by smugglers, and in 1773 a whole cargo of tea, sent to Boston direct from India at a special low rate of duty, was thrown into the harbour by colonists dressed as Indians.

The British government decided that the time had come to take action, and decided to pass an act closing Boston harbour and putting the whole state of Massachusetts under their direct control. This was a serious step, and within a year war had broken out in earnest. The colonial forces were commanded by a Virginian soldier named George Washington, who had fought with great bravery against the French. He was to prove a great general. On 4 July 1776, the thirteen colonies declared themselves to be free and independent, and in 1778 the French joined in on their side. By 1781 the last British force in America had surrendered. In 1783 the British recognized the United States of America. The greater part of the British Empire had gone, and a new

One of the first battles of the American revolution was at Bunker Hill, where British troops forced the colonists to give up their position on the hill-top dominating Boston. British losses were more than 1,000.

power had been born. Pitt did not live to see it. He died in 1778, supporting the colonists to the last.

The remnants

There was still some empire left. Apart from her lands in India, Britain still retained Canada, which had remained loyal when the colonies farther south had revolted. In addition, she owned valuable sugar islands in the West Indies, won in various wars throughout the seventeenth and eighteenth centuries. Like the southern states in America, these islands relied on slaves for their prosperity, and were very rich. Indeed, there was some talk of exchanging the whole of Canada for another of these islands. After all, Canada seemed to be a waste, completely inaccessible during the winter when the St Lawrence was frozen up, and with little of value but furs. How much more valuable was an island on an established trade route – what was more, an island producing such a valuable cash crop as sugar! Britain's statesmen were tempted, but in the end the scheme fell through, and Canada remained British. It was later found to be one of the richest countries in the world, with huge deposits of valuable minerals.

New voyages

Thus Britain had still got territory on the opposite side of the Atlantic, and in India. In addition, even as America was being lost, an English sailor who had helped to pilot Wolfe's boats to Quebec was exploring the South Pacific in search of new lands. He was a northcountryman named James Cook. A calm and gentle man, a magnificent leader, he was also one of the greatest navigators and makers of maps who have ever lived. On one great voyage, among other tasks, he mapped the whole coastline of New Zealand and the east coast of Australia. This was a difficult and dangerous task. The east coast of Australia has many perilous reefs, and Cook's ship, the *Endeavour*, was always liable to

Left: map of the routes followed by Cook on his three voyages. *Above:* portrait of Cook.

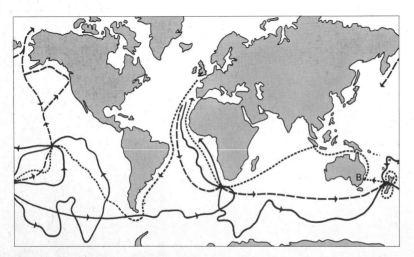

```
·············· 1st voyage
————————— 2nd voyage
— — — — — 3rd voyage
B = Botany Bay
```

126

Cook's sailors had varied experiences. *Above:* they sail among the Antarctic ice. *Centre:* they witness a native dance in Tahiti. *Below:* they shoot walruses for meat.

run aground. When the voyage was over, it was found that her keel was worn down as thin as the sole of a shoe.

Banks and Botany Bay

On board the *Endeavour* on this voyage was Joseph Banks, a man of many parts, but with a particular passion for the study of plants. It was he who named one of the bays on the coast of Australia Botany Bay, because of the huge number of plants he had found there. He was quite certain that Botany Bay was an ideal site for European settlement, and suggested that those Americans who were leaving the United States because they wished to live under British rule should be encouraged to settle there. This scheme was not really taken seriously and they eventually moved only to Canada. But Banks continued to make his point. If loyalists could not be persuaded to go to Australia, then other settlers ought to be found. Fortunately, there were plenty of people who could be sent. The prisons were full of them. For years convicts had been shipped off to the American and West Indian plantations. Now, after 1783, it was impossible to send them to America any more and the prisons in England were getting overcrowded. The government, convinced that something had to be done, decided in 1787 to try the experiment of transporting convicts to Botany Bay to see how they

Left: all that was known of New Zealand before Cook's voyages. It is marked in the bottom right-hand corner of the map. *Right:* New Zealand as charted by Cook. Notice how carefully his voyage followed the coastline so as not to miss a single feature of importance.

128

fared. The experiment was a success and transportation to Australia, for seven, fourteen years, or for life, became a common punishment for criminals. In this way, the British settlement in Australia started.

Yet Cook's voyages and the first settlements in Australia did nothing at the time to balance the loss of the American colonies. After all, Canada, the islands in the West Indies, the territories in India, and an obscure convict outpost in Australia, were all nothing when compared with the thirteen prosperous colonies that had stretched down the east coast of America. To most Britons these had been the Empire, and their loss seemed a death-blow to British hopes of establishing a great empire overseas. Pitt seemed to have lived in vain.

Dates to remember

1756   Seven Years War began
1757   Pitt took over
1761   Pitt resigned
1763   Treaty of Paris
1776   American Declaration of Independence

Things to do

1   Compare the personalities and abilities of Walpole and Pitt. To what circumstances was each best fitted? Can you think of other politicians in other ages like them?
2   Find out about the career of George Washington.
3   Find out more about the early history of the settlement of Australia.

Books to read

C. Clarke, *The American Revolution*, Longmans
R. Howard (ed.), *Wolfe at Quebec*, Cape (Jackdaw)
L. James, *A Soldier in Washington's Army*, Oxford University Press
D. Johnson (ed.), *The American Revolution*, Cape (Jackdaw)
D. Johnson (ed.), *Clive of India*, Cape (Jackdaw)
S. Lewenhak (ed.), *The Voyages of Captain Cook*, Cape (Jackdaw)
D. W. Sylvester, *Clive in India*, Longmans
O. Warner, *Captain Cook and the South Pacific*, Cassell
B. Williams, *The Struggle for Canada*, Longmans
N. Wymer, *Soldiers and Sailors* (Chapters on Wolfe and Clive), Oxford University Press

Chapter 10
Wilkes and liberty!

John Wilkes was a Whig journalist and member of Parliament. An amazingly ugly man, with a huge lop-sided jaw and a dreadful squint, he wrote very effective political articles, full of the most violent abuse of his Tory opponents. For instance, he once described one member of Parliament as 'the most treacherous, base, selfish, mean, abject, lowlived and dirty fellow that ever wriggled his way into a secretaryship'. He was never afraid to own what he had written, and was quite prepared to fight a duel with the man he had insulted, for he was no coward. He was on very good terms with many of the Whig members, for his articles were very useful to them, and, in any case, he was a charming, witty, cheerful fellow, who enjoyed all the good things of life to the full and was always excellent company.

Number 45

In the years immediately following the death of George II in 1760, Wilkes was very busy, for George III disliked and distrusted the Whigs, and tried to give more power to the Tories. This naturally annoyed the Whigs, who had ruled the country for more than sixty years. As a result, Wilkes wrote article after article in his paper – the *North Briton* – attacking the King's new ministers. When no action was taken against him, he grew bolder and bolder, claiming that he was trying to find out how far freedom of the Press extended in Britain. In 1763 he found out. As you read in the last chapter, the government decided to make peace with France, and the treaty which they signed was very unpopular with the merchants. Wilkes at once launched a most violent attack on the government in number 45 of the *North Briton*, and was arrested.

Once under arrest, Wilkes was taken for questioning to the Home Secretary, but he refused to answer any questions and made pointed comments about the pictures which the Home Secretary had hung on his walls. He was then packed off to the Tower of London, his house was searched and all his papers were taken away. Within a few days he was free again, released by a judge who said that the crime of which he was accused was not serious enough for him to have been put into prison. After all, he was a member of Parliament, and could therefore only be imprisoned on very serious charges. When he reached home from the Tower, he found his papers gone, and at once wrote to the Home Secretary:

I find that my house has been robbed and am informed that the stolen goods are in the possession of one or both of your lordships. I therefore insist that you do forthwith return them to, your humble servant, John Wilkes.

THE

NORTH BRITON

NUMBER XLV.

To be continued every *Saturday*. Price Two pence Halfpen

SATURDAY, APRIL the 23, 1763.

The following advertisement appeared in all the papers on. 13th of April.

THE NORTH BRITON makes his appeal the good sense, and to the candour of ENGLISH nation. In the present unsett and fluctuating state of the *administrati* he is really fearful of falling into involu tary errors, and he does not wish to mislead. All reasonings have been built on the strong foundation *facts*; and he is not yet informed of the whole interio state of government with such *minute precision*, as now venture the submitting his crude ideas of the present politic crisis to the discerning and impartial public. The SCO TISH minister has indeed *retired*. Is HIS influence at end? or does HE still govern by the *three* wretched too of his power, who, to their indelible infamy, have su ported the most odious of his measure, the late ignom nious *Peace*, and the wicked extension of the arbitra mode of *Excise*? The NORTH BRITON has been stea

The famous No. 45, published in 1763. It does not look very exciting compared with most present day publications, but its message was evidently clear enough.

Drawing of Wilkes by Hogarth. Hogarth did not like Wilkes and made a savage cartoon of him based on this sketch.

He then sued the government for wrongful arrest, because the warrant on which he had been arrested did not contain his name. In fact, the warrant had simply ordered the arrest of all those who had helped to produce number 45 of the *North Briton*. Wilkes claimed that such 'general warrants' were illegal. He won his case, and was paid £1,000 compensation. By now he was famous all over the country. The number 45 was chalked up on walls and doors everywhere, and all those who disliked the government were delighted with Wilkes's coolness and courage. 'Wilkes and Liberty' became the popular cry.

Wilkes in exile

But disaster was not far away. First, when Parliament met, the Commons condemned number 45. During the debate, a government supporter named Samuel Martin, who had been attacked in the *North Briton*, made a violent personal attack on Wilkes, describing him as 'a cowardly

This eighteenth-century pistol is a flintlock. When the trigger is pulled the piece of flint in the hammer strikes a spark off the metal plate in front of it. This fires the charges by igniting a small quantity of powder over a hole leading down into the barrel.

rascal, a villain and a scoundrel'. He then sent him a letter, in which he wrote, 'I desire that you meet me in Hyde Park immediately with a brace of pistols each, to determine our differences'. Wilkes's friends knew that Martin had been practising pistol-shooting for weeks past, and advised Wilkes to reject the challenge, but he insisted on accepting it and was very severely wounded. As soon as he was well enough, he went to France to visit his daughter, and, while he was there, a warrant was issued for his arrest. When he failed to come forward, he was outlawed and expelled from the House of Commons. His career seemed to be at an end, and he remained quietly in France.

The Middlesex elections

In 1768, however, to the astonishment of all, he returned to England to stand for Parliament again. First, he stood for London, but was defeated, so transferred to Middlesex. With the help of two friends,

Wilkes *(centre)* and his two helpers, Glynn, the lawyer *(left)*, Horne Tooke, the parson *(right)*, painted in 1768.

Glynn, a lawyer, and Horne Tooke, a clever, drunken parson, he organized an election campaign. He visited the electors, distributed pamphlets, and made speeches. Once again the number 45 appeared on walls and doors, and Wilkes's unmistakable face was pictured on every public house. 'Squints', said one admirer, 'Well, if he does, it is no more than a man should squint.' The freeholders of Middlesex were carefully organized and, on polling day, Wilkes was elected with 1,292 votes – 400 more than either of the other two candidates. He had lost none of his old popularity, and for two days London went mad, with mobs roaming the streets forcing all and sundry to give a cheer for Wilkes and Liberty.

Meanwhile Wilkes himself was in prison, arrested on the warrant which had been issued while he was in France. He was charged with writing number 45 of the *North Briton* and other works, and was sentenced to twenty-two months in prison. His stay was comfortable.

Perhaps the greatest tribute the people could pay to a politician was to unharness the horses from his coach and drag it along themselves. Wilkes was so honoured in 1768.

Indeed, it was a sort of triumph. He had pleasant rooms, could have as many visitors as he liked, and could go where he pleased in the building. What was more, his supporters sent him huge quantities of food and drink and while he was in prison he was even elected an alderman of the City of London! But the government decided that they would not have him as a member of the House of Commons, and in February 1769 he was expelled, and a new election was ordered. To the annoyance of the government, he was once again elected. Indeed, nobody bothered to stand against him. Once again they expelled him from the House, and declared that he was 'incapable of being elected a member'. This was a challenge which Wilkes could not resist. At the next election, his name was put forward yet again. Yet again he was elected. The government candidate, Luttrell, polled only 296 votes against over 1,100 for Wilkes. None the less, the House of Commons declared Luttrell elected.

Who elects the members?

Meanwhile, support for Wilkes was growing. For one thing, he and his friends did something quite new. Instead of looking on their electors as being simply there to vote them in, and then be forgotten until the next election, Wilkes's friends met them at regular intervals to find out what they wanted their members to do. This made Wilkes very popular among the Middlesex electors, who were very annoyed that he was expelled from the House of Commons. Apart from this, Wilkes's supporters were touring the country, persuading people to send petitions to the government to allow Wilkes to sit. They did their job well, and petitions flowed in from all over the country. The fact was that many people were uneasy at what the government was doing. It seemed to them that in saying that Wilkes could not sit, the ministers were almost claiming the right to elect their members for them. It seemed a very dangerous step and opposition to the government grew steadily. Finally the great Pitt himself spoke up for Wilkes in Parliament and the Prime Minister, overwhelmed by the strength of the opposition, resigned.

The secrets of Parliament

The new Prime Minister was a Tory, Lord North, a very good-natured man, entirely under George III's influence. Almost at the same time, Wilkes came out of prison after serving his sentence. Within a year, he was in trouble again, this time over printing the debates of the House of Commons. Today, we take it for granted that the electors have the right to know what goes on in Parliament, but in the eighteenth century the House of Commons were anxious to keep their debates as secret as they could. They thought that the members ought to be able to say what they liked without having to bother about what people outside Parliament thought. After all, it was Parliament's job to govern. Anyway, in 1770 it was illegal to print accounts of debates, and George and his ministers were determined to enforce the law. Accordingly, a printer who had published accounts of debates was arrested and brought before three London magistrates. The outlook for him seemed black.

Fortunately for him, however, the magistrates were in fact Wilkes and two of his friends. They heard the case, and immediately ordered the release of the printer, who, they said, had committed no crime. The House of Commons were furious, and ordered two of the magistrates to be imprisoned in the Tower. In addition, they ordered Wilkes to appear before them. Wilkes refused, and the government realized that they had gone too far. The magistrates were released, and the case was dropped. Since then debates have been printed without any interference.

Wilkes and London

By 1771 Wilkes was an important figure in the government of the City of London. He was elected Sheriff, and finally Lord Mayor, which gave him a good deal of power in the City. He used this power to good effect

This ceremony, involving the Lord Mayor and Aldermen of the City of London, took place in 1782. The wealth and importance of the city is reflected in the splendours of the hall. Wilkes is seated *(right)* among the Aldermen.

This engraving, by Hogarth, shows some of the cruelties which Wilkes tried to prevent.

to help those least able to help themselves. He lowered the price of bread, inspected the London prisons to make sure that debtors were not being ill-treated, stopped prisoners being brought into court in irons and declared it illegal for press gangs to carry men off against their will to serve in the navy. He was even concerned for the suffering of animals, trying to stop cruelty to cattle in Smithfield market. Where he had no power to act himself, he tried to persuade others to do something, telling the Home Secretary that too many offences were punished by the death penalty, and trying, without success, to get his support to reduce their number. So strong was Wilkes's position that when he was once more elected by the people of Middlesex as their member, the government allowed him to take his seat in the Commons without any trouble.

Wilkes in the Commons

Once back in the Commons, Wilkes went on where he had left off, attacking the King and his ministers at every opportunity. He began by suggesting that 30 January, the anniversary of the execution of Charles I, should be celebrated as a festival, not kept as a fast, and in a later debate he complained, with some justice, that taxes were being used to bribe members of Parliament to vote as the King wished. In another debate he pointed out that 254 members of the Commons were elected by a total of only 5,732 voters, 'generally the inhabitants of Cornish and other insignificant boroughs'. This was a deliberate insult to the King, for many of these Cornish boroughs were on Royal estates, and George could always rely on them to return members who agreed with his point of view. Wilkes even went so far as to suggest that an act should be passed taking the members from the small boroughs, and giving them to the large towns, many of which had no representatives in Parliament at all. What was more, he proposed that the right to vote should be given to 'the meanest mechanic, the poorest peasant and day labourer'. Nobody in the Commons took such revolutionary suggestions seriously.

Wilkes and the American colonies

But they had to take some of his speeches seriously, especially those concerning America. Wilkes had always been a supporter of the colonists against the government and when the war started in 1775, he made speech after speech, calling the war 'unjust, felonious and murderous'. When the colonists declared themselves independent in 1776, he at once began referring to them as 'the free and independent states of America', pouring scorn on those who thought that Britain had any chance of defeating them. Nor was Wilkes alone in this campaign. Edmund Burke, a great Irish orator, supported the colonists in the Commons, while in the Lords, Pitt, though broken by age and illness, poured out a magnificent torrent of eloquence on behalf of the Americans. As you have read, it was all to no avail, and the war dragged on until 1783 when North had to admit final defeat. It was the end of his ministry, for the Commons could not trust a minister who allowed his country to be defeated in a war against its own colonies.

Wilkes loses his power

North was not the only politician to suffer as a result of the war with America. So did Wilkes. He was only really powerful because he was popular among people prosperous and influential enough to have votes. When he stood up in Parliament and spoke in favour of the Americans, against whom Englishmen were fighting, he was speaking against the feelings of most Englishmen, for the country was properous and the war was popular. This lost him much important support and the Gordon riots of 1780, described in the next chapter, put an end to his popularity

Destruction of Newgate by the Gordon rioters in 1780. Outside they make a bonfire of the contents.

in London once and for all. Wilkes was horrified at the violence of the mob and thought it was his duty to restore order. He therefore ordered troops to fire on seething crowds to disperse them. The crowds went home disillusioned. They never again turned out to cheer him.

Wilkes and Johnson

The fact that Wilkes no longer had the support of the mob did not make him miserable. He simply became respectable. He even met and talked with George III, who was amazed at his civility. Indeed, he could still use his charm with great effect even on those who detested his very name and all he stood for. Such a man was Samuel Johnson, the great author. Born in Lichfield, Johnson was among the greatest writers of his age. He is famous as the compiler of the first English dictionary, but he wrote many poems and books as well. His style is still admired for its elegance and balance, and in his day he was one of the most famous men in London. A huge, clumsy, shambling sort of man, he was the centre of a large circle of friends, who included David Garrick, the great Shakespearean actor, Sir Joshua Reynolds, the painter, Oliver Goldsmith, the playwright, Dr Burney, the musician, and a young Scot named James Boswell, who delighted in meeting famous men, and afterwards wrote Johnson's life.

Johnson dominated this group. His learning was immense, and his tongue was often rough. He had decided views on most things, and they were almost all opposed to those of Wilkes. Where Wilkes was a violent Whig, Johnson was a High Tory, and had, indeed, written a pamphlet against Wilkes in the years gone by. Wilkes supported the Americans: Johnson hated them. Wilkes had no use for the monarchy: Johnson held it in great respect. Wilkes was a merry jesting fellow: Johnson was serious and melancholy. Two men more opposite to each other it is difficult to imagine, yet Boswell was determined that they should meet. Eventually he arranged that they were both invited to the same dinner-

Below: some of Johnson's friends. The portrait of Boswell is by Reynolds.

David Garrick

Sir Joshua Reynolds

Oliver Goldsmith

James Boswell

An eighteenth-century coffee house. The coffee pots are in a row in front of the fire, and the coffee is served in bowls.

Johnson (right) taking tea. He described himself as 'A hardened and shameless tea drinker'.

party. Johnson was the last guest to arrive, and was rather taken aback to see Wilkes there. He therefore took a book from his pocket, retired to a window seat and sat there reading. He was determined to have nothing to do with his fellow-guest if he could help it.

Leicester Square, London, in the eighteenth century. It was then a quiet residential district. It has changed since.

In fact Johnson succeeded in avoiding Wilkes until the dinner was served. Then, to his dismay, he found Wilkes sitting next to him. To cap it all, the squinting old fellow turned to him with a smile and began, with great good manners, to help him to some meat. 'Pray give me leave, sir – it is better here – a little of the brown? – Some fat, sir? A little of the stuffing? – some gravy? – Let me have the pleasure of giving you some butter. Allow me to recommend a squeeze of this orange – or the lemon, perhaps, may have more zest.' Johnson, who loved his food, was quite overcome by all this attention. 'Sir, sir, I am obliged to you, sir,' he said and soon he and Wilkes were chatting amiably about details of Latin poetry, and making jokes against the Scots. Wilkes's charm had worked again, and when Johnson left, he remarked how pleased he had been with Mr Wilkes's company!

The extinct volcano

Wilkes could look back on a useful life. Besides making life easier for many people in London, he had made sure that nobody could be arrested unless their name was actually on the warrant. He had established the principle that it is the electors and not the government who decide who shall sit in the House of Commons and he helped to make possible the printing of Parliamentary debates. In the past he had never been afraid to speak up on the unpopular side, but now he took things more easily. To those who tried to get his support for some reform, he

This splendid George III coin was the first copper penny to be minted in England. It weighs an ounce, and was struck by Matthew Boulton in Birmingham in 1797.

simply replied, 'I am an extinct volcano', and passed on. After the fall of North in 1783, Wilkes saw Pitt's young son, William, become Prime Minister. William was only twenty-four, but he set about the task of bringing the country up to date with great courage and skill. The taxation system was reformed, dishonesty was checked, prosperity increased and all seemed set for many years of peace and contentment. Wilkes could afford to relax.

Dates to remember

1763   Number 45 of the *North Briton*
1768   Wilkes stood for Middlesex
1774   Wilkes allowed to take his seat

Things to do

Try to find out some more about Johnson and his friends.

Things to discuss

What is there about Wilkes's policies that makes him seem a very 'modern' politician?

Books to Read

J. Dymoke, *London in the Eighteenth Century*, Longman

The 'with-it' young men of the eighteenth century were called 'macaronis'. They are drinking asses' milk sold in the street.

Chapter 11
The coming of Methodism

The Wesley family

At the end of 1707, Samuel Wesley was a poor parson, Rector of Epworth in Lincolnshire. He had a troubled life. Only two years earlier, he had been in a debtors' prison at Lincoln because he owed money to members of his congregation. Now his wife was expecting their eighteenth child. If they had all survived, he could never have managed to feed and clothe them, but nine of them had died young. Even so, it had been a struggle, for Wesley was careless about money. Fortunately, the two boys who survived were intelligent lads. The elder, Samuel, was already King's scholar at Westminster School, and young John, only four, already showed he would be able to make his way in the world. Now, in 1707, these two were joined by another brother, Charles. He very nearly joined his nine brothers and sisters in the churchyard straight away, for he was born eight weeks before his time, and was a weak and shrunken child. In the end, however, he survived.

A public school education

There was never any doubt what the three boys were to do for a living – they were to be clergymen. Like Samuel, John and Charles both went away to school after winning scholarships. John went to Charterhouse, and Charles to Westminster. Here they worked hard. At Westminster, they were roused at five, had prayers at six, and then began lessons in Greek and Latin. These lasted until about eleven, when they had a large meal, during which they listened to the reading

A village school. There was little or no money available for such schools.

of a Latin manuscript. After this, more lessons until six in the evening, then another meal, an hour's translation from English into Latin, and bed at eight o'clock. You might think this day long enough without any extra work, but many boys, in fact, worked far into the night. As a result, they used to drop off to sleep during lessons the next day, and were usually allowed to have a nap of a quarter of an hour or so to freshen their minds. There were no organized games and no holidays, only in the summer the school moved from Westminster to College House at Chiswick for a few months.

It was a hard life, and discipline was strict, being enforced by frequent floggings. Not that this stopped mischief. The boys were always fighting each other and one, the young Duke of Richmond, set fire to the hair of one of his teachers and then boxed his ears to put it out again! Charles stayed at Westminster until he was seventeen, and then followed his brother John to Oxford, on a scholarship. Here, unlike many, he worked hard, and was ready to be ordained. His elder brother was already a clergyman, and was acting as curate to their father at Epworth.

The Church in the eighteenth century

The Church which these young men were entering was in a poor state. Many of the clergy were underpaid, and a large proportion of those who had good livings did not seem really interested in religion. Like the Wesleys, they had always taken it for granted that they would go into the Church, and just looked on being a clergyman as a way of getting a living, which was to be enjoyed as much as possible. A French traveller in England in 1695, wrote how surprising it was to see most of the clergy looking so healthy and prosperous. 'It is', he wrote, 'a pleasure to look at all these fat and rosy chaplains. These gentlemen are accused of being rather lazy, and their round bellies make one suspect that there is something in this. Besides, they are found in the coffee houses, their

Westminster College was much richer.

Yet even Westminster had only one school room. At least six classes are in session at once.

pipes in their hands, and often, too, in the taverns.' Nearly a hundred years later, a Swiss clergyman travelling in England was very shocked to find a room in a tavern in Oxford full of clergymen, 'all with their gowns and bands on, sitting round a table, each with his pot of beer before him.' They were occupied in teasing each other with quotations from the Bible until the party was broken up after midnight, by one of them starting up, shouting 'Damn me, I must read prayers this morning at All Souls'. Nor was it only foreigners who were critical. An Englishman described the clergy as 'fine gentlemen, who are far more anxious to attain the fame of being excellent shots, giving the view hallo, well mounted in the field, and being in at the death, than raising their voices at the desk or pulpit, or feeding the flock, whom they are eager to fleece.'

Parson Woodforde

Of course there were clergymen who did a good job, even if they were not really dedicated to the life. Such a one was James Woodforde, rector of Weston Longville in Norfolk. He kept a diary, which gives a good picture of the life he led. He had a fine church, and an income of £400 a year. He was unmarried, and kept five servants and three horses. He was on very good terms with the squire and the neighbouring clergy, and was generous to the poor of his parish. For instance, on Christmas Day, he used to entertain them to a dinner of beef followed by plum pudding,

A church interior by Hogarth. Notice the 'three decker' pulpit, the galleries, the organ, and the box pews.

How a cartoonist saw the
Church of England parson,
returning from tything.

and then send them away with a shilling each. At other times he sent
them presents of food, and if any were ill, he would do his best to provide some delicacy for them. On the other hand, he employed a smuggler
to bring him tea, went to see an execution, used to attend bear-
baitings, and was fond of fishing, dancing and going to the theatre. But
above all, Woodforde liked his food. Once, when he entertained four
guests, he provided 'a leg of mutton boiled and capers, a boiled fowl and
a tongue, a batter pudding, a fine turkey roasted, fried rabbits, tarts,
custards and jellies. Almonds, raisins, oranges and apples after. Port
wine, mountain, porter and ale, etc.' It is no wonder that he was sometimes anxious as to whether he ate too much!

Woodforde, then, was interested above all in the things of this world.
He preached regularly, and gave help to those who needed it, but he
did not think it any part of his duty to go out to try to convert people
to Christianity. If they came to church, he preached them a sermon; if
they did not, he left them alone. Most of the congregation were respectable people, many of whom paid regular pew-rents for their seats in
church, and this was how the parson liked it. As a result, the Church of
England was losing touch with the working people of England.

Gin Lane

This was particularly true in the towns. Take, for instance, London.
The great mass of Londoners never went to school, could therefore
neither read nor write and never went near a church. Religion was only
for their betters. They appeared to have no morals at all, and were
brutal and violent. They were perhaps at their worst between 1700 and
1751, when cheap gin was available in vast quantities from between
6,000 and 7,000 'dram shops'. For twopence you could drink until you
fell, and then have your sleep out on clean straw at no extra charge.
Such a hold did gin-drinking get, that some workmen were paid in gin,
rather than in money, and Acts of Parliament which tried to control it

145

had no effect, for nobody dared to enforce them. By 1742 the consumption of gin had reached 7,000,000 gallons a year, which was just over a gallon per head of the population. What was more, the death-rate in London, where most was drunk, was higher than anywhere else in the country, and much higher than the birth-rate. In addition, the spirits tended to make people more desperate and violent than ever. Eventually the conscience of the country was roused, partly by the picture 'Gin Lane' by Hogarth, which you will find reproduced opposite. This, which was widely circulated, so shocked people that Parliament at last passed an effective act to limit sales.

But even later in the century, the London mob was still capable of frightful brutality. In 1771, for instance, a mob of 2,000 pelted an informer with brick ends for three hours, only stopping when he died. Nine years later the mob broke out again. In 1778 an act was passed by Parliament, making it possible for Catholics to own land, and allowing their priests to come into the country. Some Protestants were very alarmed at this, and got up a petition to Parliament, asking them to repeal the act. When the petition was presented to Parliament in 1780, it gave rise to the Gordon riots in which a huge mob took control of the whole city for a week, burning and looting. There was no police force to control them, and though troops were called in, nobody wanted to take the responsibility to tell them to open fire. As a result, the mob did as they pleased, and there was a real reign of terror.

Perhaps the most dreadful scenes occurred when the mob fired a gin distillery. One cobbler took over a fire engine, and used it to pump gin into buckets, to sell at a penny a mug.

Others, unwilling to pay for what they could get for nothing, ran into the raging building and down the stone steps into the cellar and came up choking with blackened faces and bloodshot eyes, carrying untapped casks of gin, or pails and jugs, bowls and even pig troughs overflowing . . . Soon the stills

Gin Lane from an engraving by Hogarth in 1751. The only prosperous buildings are those of the pawnbroker, the undertaker, and the gin distiller. The rest are tumbledown. A mother lets her child fall to its death; a workman pawns the tools of his trade; a drunken mob riots; one man, in despair, hangs himself.

In Beer Street, on the other hand, all are prosperous, contented, and hardworking, with almost superhuman strength. Only the pawnbroker's house is in ruins.

burst and overflowed and the gin came gushing up into the streets and ran in warm streams in the gutter. Delirious with excitement, the people knelt down and dipped their faces in the river of fiery spirits and gulped as much of it down as they could before it made them choke. For the gin was in its raw state, unrectified. Wraxall saw men and women lying down prostrate in the streets, incapably drunk; some of the women had babies in their arms or struggling near their insensible bodies, screaming in terror or in pain.

Many got drunk in the cellars, and were burned to death there, shouting and laughing. During the week, more than 800 people were killed, and hundreds of thousands of pounds worth of damage was done. It was a dreadful experience.

These riots were, of course, exceptional, even for London, but violence was never far away in any town. You will read how mobs destroyed new inventions and tried to kill the inventors in the cloth towns, and have seen the way in which crowds behaved at elections. Such people lived in a different world from Woodforde, placidly sitting in his rectory, writing in his diary about that day's dinner, nor was he bothered about them. Why should he be? They were not in his parish.

John and Charles start work

From the very beginning John and Charles Wesley did not fit in with men like Woodforde. For one thing, they thought seriously about their religion, and discussed it with others, and for another, they went

Portrait of John Wesley, painted in 1766.

visiting prisons to comfort the prisoners. So serious and methodical were they, that they became known as 'Methodists', and tended to be figures of fun. They decided to try to make a career in the colonies but returned to England after only a short stay. In England, they continued their discussions and studies, in some doubt as to what they should do. Suddenly, in 1739, both of them saw that all they had to do was to have faith in Christ, and all would be well. This gave them such peace of mind that they thought it was their duty to go and preach their faith all over the country. From then on, wherever they went, they talked to people, trying to get them to believe in the power of Christ to save them, however wicked they might have been. For instance, Charles Wesley wrote of a coach journey to London, during which he preached to his fellow-passengers, telling them to have faith in Christ. 'A lady', he remarked, 'was extremely offended: avowed her own merits in plain terms: asked if I was not a Methodist: threatened to beat me. I declared, I deserved nothing but Hell: so did she: and must confess it, before she could have a title to Heaven. This was most intolerable to her.'

But it was not only in coaches that the Wesleys preached. They continued to visit prisons, and comforted those condemned to hang, with the news – and it was news to many of them – that Christ had died to save them too. More than this, they rode up and down the country, preaching everywhere in the open air. Charles wrote hymns, many of

A Methodist minister preaching in the open air in 1777. This habit attracted those who did not as a rule go to church.

National Gallery of Canada, Ottawa

which have become famous, which the congregation could sing before the sermon, and then either John or Charles would preach, telling the crowd that Christianity was for them too, if only they would believe. They knew no parish boundaries – 'The world is my parish', said John Wesley, and they soon became well known. Their reception varied. Usually, the local clergy were against them, and sometimes organized a mob to try to frighten them away. They never succeeded, for the Methodists welcomed the opportunity to talk to the mob about religion.

The first Methodist Chapel, set up in a disused foundry in 1739. Besides the chapel, which would hold 1,500 people, the foundry also contained a school and preacher's house.

The movement grows

The Wesleys were soon joined by others, the most famous of whom was Whitefield, who afterwards broke with them, because they could not agree about their beliefs. Soon, their sermons became famous, and, wherever they or their followers went, they could be sure of a crowd. In Wales, where the Church of England's hold was especially weak, they made a huge number of converts, though even there all was not peaceful. In 1740, some Methodists went to Caerleon.

'At first,' wrote one of them,

it seemed as if we were to have peace, but after we had sung, prayed and discoursed for half an hour, the crowd became hostile, and pelted us even worse than they had at Newport. The Lord gave us sufficient strength to hold on for an hour and a half. Sometimes we sang hymns in the midst of the turmoil,

This chapel, in City Road London, was erected in 1820, and specifically designed as a chapel. Its lines are much simpler than those of a church.

but our voices were drowned by the noise. At last I was struck by a stone, or piece of brick, or some other hard substance on my right eye. This gave me such excruciating pain that I was forced to return to the tavern and give up preaching.

At Monmouth, their preaching was drowned by the beating of a large drum, they were showered with nuts and plum stones, and a fire engine was turned on to them, only it did not work. But still they preached on. In the end, the writer of the above account was killed by a stone thrown by one of a mob to whom he was preaching at Hay-on-Wye, only a few months later.

The leopards are laid down

Often, however, the crowd's hostility was stilled by the personality of the preachers, and their message got through. At Bolton, Charles Wesley went to the house of a brother Methodist, on hearing that an angry mob had broken into it. He wrote,

I walked down into the thickest of them. I called for a chair. The winds were hushed, and all was calm and still. My heart was filled with love, my eye with tears, and my mouth with arguments. They were annoyed, they were ashamed, they were melted down, they devoured every word.

On another occasion he met a party of 1,000 miners on their way to

Bristol to start a riot. He persuaded them instead to put their grievances to the Mayor peacefully, and then return. They did so. 'All who saw', he wrote, 'were amazed, for the leopards were laid down.'

Undoubtedly the Methodists did much good. They were often mocked because they were so enthusiastic and trusting that they sometimes made themselves ridiculous. On the other hand, many people had their lives transformed by their preaching, for they gave hope and faith to those who had neither, and who had been ignored by the Church of England. People now felt that they had something to live for, apart from gin, and mended their lives accordingly. What was more, they always taught that violence was wrong, and that Christians should always obey the government. Some historians have even gone so far as to say that their preaching prevented a violent revolution from breaking out in England. Certainly they converted thousands to a faith which made them better citizens. But in doing this, they had to leave the Church of England, because it did not approve of the way in which they preached out of church. They therefore set up a Church of their own, with a separate organization, which still exists today.

Dates to remember

1703   John Wesley born
1791   John Wesley died

Things to do

1   Find out when the Methodist Church in your area was founded.
2   Find out as many popular hymns written by Charles Wesley as you can.
3   Try to find out if the Wesleys visited your part of the country. Were there any other famous preachers who lived and worked in your district during the eighteenth century? If so, find out something about them.

Things to discuss

Read the following extracts, and then discuss why Methodism was so unpopular among the aristocracy, and so popular among more humble people.

The first is from a letter written by the Duchess of Buckingham to Lady Huntingdon.

I thank Your Ladyship for the information concerning the Methodist preachers; their doctrines are most repulsive and strongly tinctured with impertinence and disrespect towards their Superiors, in perpetually endeavouring to level all ranks and do away with all distinctions. It is monstrous to be told you have a heart as sinful as the common wretches that crawl on the earth. This is highly offensive and insulting and I cannot but wonder that Your ladyship should relish any sentiments so much at variance with Good Breeding and High Rank.

Now here is William Clowes describing what it was like to be converted by a Methodist preacher.

The power of Heaven came down upon me and I cried for help to Him who is mighty to save. It was towards the close of the meeting when I felt my bands breaking, and when the change was taking place. I thought within myself, What is this? This, I said, is what the Methodists mean by being converted. Yes, God is converting my soul. In an agony of prayer I believed he would save me. Then I believed he was saving me. Then I believed he had saved me. And it was so.

Another, Hugh Bourne, wrote:

In an instant I had power over sin which I had not before, and I was filled with joy and glory which made full amends for the twenty years' suffering. The Bible looked new, and I felt a love to all mankind, and my desire was that friends and enemies and all the world might be saved.

Books to read

J. Kazantzis (ed.), *The Gordon Riots*, Cape (Jackdaw)
D. Marshall, *John Wesley*, Oxford University Press
R. Whately, *A Charity School Boy*, Oxford University Press

Travel by sedan chair through a boisterous crowd in Covent Garden.

Chapter 12
Village life in the eighteenth century

William's home

In 1780 William Wilkins lived in a small village in Nottinghamshire. He was a farmer and was now fifty years old. He had a wife and two children. His son, John, aged nineteen, worked on the Squire's land when he was not helping his father. His daughter Alice, who was sixteen, helped Mrs Wilkins look after the hens and milk the cow and spent the rest of her time spinning raw wool into thread on their spinning wheel. William was far from rich. He had only a little land and a small cottage, built of timber framing filled in with brick. The doors and windows fitted none too well and in the winter draughts howled across the floor and up the huge chimney of the living-room. To keep warm William and his family would sit on the hearth itself, which was so big that there was room for four people to sit in comfort on benches with very high backs to keep off the draught. Not that William had much time for sitting about, for he and his family had to work hard to get enough to live on. But he was independent and was proud of the fact

Photograph of the main room in an old cottage. The fire is used for cooking as well as heating the room.

that his family had lived in the same cottage and farmed their own land for as long as anyone could remember. He could just read and write, but rarely did either. He had never been far from his village, for he was too poor to own a horse, so that his wanderings were limited to the distance he could walk in a day, which was about twenty miles.

Squire and Rector

The two most important people in the village were the Squire and the Rector. The Squire, whose ancestors had been Squires for as long as William's family had been farmers, lived in a huge house in its own grounds a little way from the centre of the village. His life was a closed book to William, who only knew of what went on at the Hall at second or third hand through some of the farmers who had daughters working as servants there. To William the Squire represented wealth and power. The Squire was a magistrate, before whom any of the villagers who were caught poaching were taken. He was an officer in the Yeomanry as well as lord of the manor. He owned a coach, and had many horses. He often went to London and had once even been to the King's Court. He frequently entertained other gentry at the Hall to huge meals washed down, so the rumour went, with gallons of port. His main amusement was hunting – a sport which William loved too, though while the Squire followed the hounds on horseback, William followed on foot. There were stories that the Squire had been a great gambler in his

The sort of house in which the lord of the manor might have lived, altered and added to as the years passed.

youth, but now he was old he rarely played cards, and then only for small stakes. For several months he had been far from well and everyone in the village was very sorry, for he had always been ready with help for those who fell on hard times.

His most frequent visitor these days was the Rector, whom he had appointed to the living nearly thirty years before. In years gone by the Squire had, like the rest of the villagers, attended church regularly and, like the rest of the villagers, he had sometimes nodded off to sleep during the sermon. Not that the rest of the congregation knew, for his pew with its embroidered cushions and leather-bound books was discreetly curtained off from the rest of the church. Perhaps the Rector knew, but he did not seem to mind, for he remained on the best of terms with the Squire, frequently dining at the Hall. Of course there were some people who pointed out that the parson could hardly reprimand the man who had given him such a good job. His glebe land was extensive and of good quality, and the tithes came in without much difficulty. The rectory was a very comfortable house, and the Rector lived well. He had two servants – and a good horse. Of late he had left a good deal of the work to his curate and was growing stout and middle aged.

So much for the two most important inhabitants of the village. For the rest, they were mostly farmers, like William, though many of them had more land and a better house than he had. On the other hand, there were one or two cottagers with no land to speak of, who relied

An eighteenth-century labouring family set out for work. At harvest time there was work for the whole family, either cutting and binding, pitching the sheaves on to the wagons, or gleaning. The labourer carries his tools – and his drink – with him. To judge by their clothes times were bad.

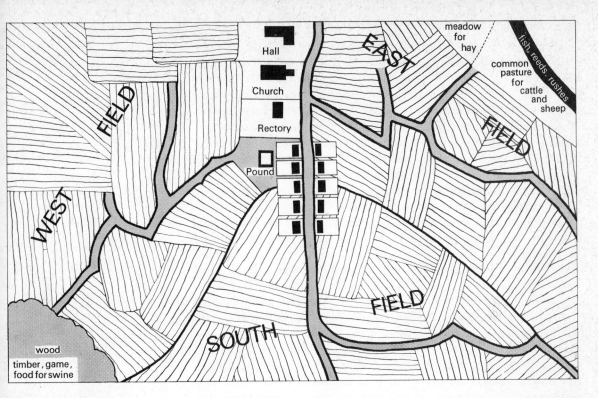

Labels on map:
Hall
Church
Rectory
Pound
WEST FIELD
EAST FIELD
SOUTH FIELD
meadow for hay
common pasture for cattle and sheep
fish, reeds, rushes
wood
timber, game, food for swine

Plan of a village before enclosure. The village is a compact unit. The pound is for stray animals. Odd corners too small to plough were used to grow hay.

almost entirely for their living on a few animals they grazed on the village pasture. Apart from this, they did casual work on other people's farms and by these means just managed to eke out a living, though they were quite unable to save anything for their old age and usually ended up in an almshouse.

The village

The village in which these people lived had changed very little in the past hundred years or so. It consisted basically of a single street, with farmhouses on either side of it. At one end stood the church and the rectory and beyond the church stood the Hall. At each end of the village, the street led into the huge open fields, which had been farmed by the villagers for almost a thousand years. There were three of these fields, each of about 350 acres. They were divided into strips, about ten yards wide and 220 yards long. William had twenty-one of these strips, seven in each field, widely scattered. In addition he had the right to graze a few animals on the common pastureland which lay beyond the open fields. All the other people in the village held their land in the same way. Of course, many of them had much more land than William. The Squire had more than a hundred strips, and the Rector more than fifty. Other wealthy farmers had nearly as many, but all, rich or poor, farmed side by side on the same land, using the same methods, with no hedge or wall to separate their holdings.

Strip farming

William's whole life was centred on this small village with its three great fields, which he knew as well as his garden. Farming in the village was a co-operative affair. It had to be when everyone's land was together. Each year one field grew winter-sown wheat, another spring wheat, while the third was left fallow to recover its fertility after having grown crops two years running and to provide additional grazing for the animals. At ploughing time the poorer farmers clubbed together to make up the team of six or eight oxen which dragged the heavy wooden plough through the soil, and all the farmers co-operated after the lambing to round up and count their sheep.

Admittedly, the system had its drawbacks. It was impossible to drain your land properly when none of the surrounding places belonged to you. The seed was sown broadcast and was sometimes almost choked with weeds, especially if the farmer who owned the next strip did not take any trouble to keep his weeds down. Moreover, there was a terrible shortage of winter feed for the cattle, which were thin, long-legged creatures, bred only for milk and for use as draught animals. Any attempts to improve the breed were doomed to failure as long as all the animals wandered together on the pasture and disease spread quickly among them. What was more, some people thought it a terrible waste to leave a third of the land uncultivated each year and pointed out what a waste of time it was to have to walk so far from one strip to another.

William accepted all these disadvantages as part of his life. He had no real wish to alter anything. Although he did not own many strips and could not keep many animals on the pasture, he could stand and look at the great expanse of land surrounding the village, without a hedge in sight, and feel that it all belonged to the community in which he lived. Wherever he wandered on those fields, he was not really trespassing. Moreover, the village was compact. All the farmhouses stood along the

The harvest is being gathered in the open fields. It is a co-operative job, with several farmers clubbing together to provide the necessary horses, carts, and labour.

158

Above: Jethro Tull.
Above right: Tull's seed drill.
The triangular boxes were
filled with seeds, and as the
wheels rotated they operated
a catch mechanism which
allowed a steady trickle of
seed into the ground.

Turnip Townshend. He was a
politician before he took up
farming.

street in the middle of the fields, no more than a few hundred yards
apart and people could easily meet and talk any time of the day. Finally,
William had enough to live on. He would never be rich, but nor would
he starve. He sold some of his corn and the wool from his sheep for
ready cash, and for the rest he lived on what he produced for himself.

Changes in farming

But in 1780, William was a worried man. If what he had heard was
true, his whole way of life was about to be destroyed and there was
nothing he could do about it. The reasons for this went a long way
back. Nearly eighty years before a Berkshire farmer, named Jethro
Tull, had noticed that all crops, including corn, grew much better if
they were properly spaced out and if the soil around them was regularly
hoed, as this kept down the weeds and let air and rain get down to the
roots. The trouble was that when seed was sown broadcast, it fell in
such confusion that it was impossible to hoe it, and difficult to weed
it at all. Tull got over this difficulty by inventing a seed drill, which
was really a box on wheels with pipes leading from it into the ground.
The box was filled with seed, and the whole contraption was pulled
along by a horse. The seed fell down the pipes into the ground as it
went along, making neat, evenly spaced rows which could easily be hoed,
and the yield of corn was increased. To make things easier still, Tull
also invented a horse hoe.

Turnip Townshend

Tull's inventions were only the start. All through the eighteenth century new discoveries and improvements were being made. Viscount
Townshend popularised the discovery that if you grew turnips and
clover in the years between the two corn crops, there was no need to
leave the land fallow every third year. The turnips provided winter
food for the livestock, and this new 'Norfolk Rotation', as it was called,

159

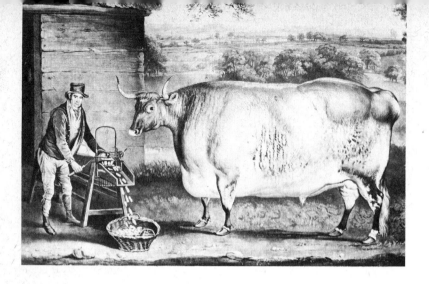

became quite well known and, where it was used, it increased the output
from the land and thus made the farmers richer. Nor was this all, for
later in the century a Leicestershire farmer named Robert Bakewell,
set about trying to improve the local strain of sheep, which were only
kept for their wool and were long legged and thin. By careful selective
breeding, he eventually produced the New Leicester, a short-legged sheep
which, as well as wool, carried a quantity of fat mutton. He also bred
good horses but his experiments with cattle were less successful. A Suffolk
farmer, Arthur Young, whose own farm was a complete failure, went
from place to place finding out all about the new methods and writing
books and articles about them, pointing out the increased production and
wealth which could be got by using them.

Now up to 1780, all this had passed William by. He could not afford
a seed drill and it was difficult to introduce a fourfold rotation of crops
with only three fields. As for improving his cattle and sheep by selective

The artist was trying to show
how fat properly bred and fed
pigs could be, but he surely
went a bit too far.

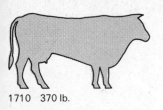

1710 370 lb.

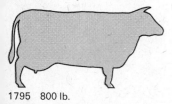

1795 800 lb.

Increase in the weight of cattle.

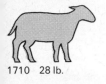

1710 28 lb.

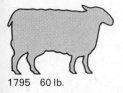

1795 60 lb.

Increase in the weight of sheep.

breeding, this was out of the question. To him all this talk of new methods and improvements had been so much hot air. But now he was not so sure. The old Squire was too set in his ways to bother with new methods, but his son, who would succeed him, was young and go-ahead. William was anxious about what he might do when he stepped into his father's shoes. He felt sure that he would want to make as much money as he could out of his land, and William knew for a fact that he had kept himself up to date with all the latest improvements and had travelled round the country to see for himself the difference they made. What was more, he never seemed to be so concerned about the welfare of the villagers as his father did.

Enclosures

In the spring of 1780 the old Squire died, and William found his worst fears realized. The new Squire was quite sure that if only he could introduce all the new ideas he had seen, he would make much more money, and went and persuaded the richer farmers in the village that they stood to gain as well. If only each man's land was all grouped together, then it would be quite easy for a rich farmer to use machinery, drain and improve his land, grow new crops on whatever system he thought fit and improve the breed of his animals. As things stood it was, of course, impossible.

Fortunately for the rich farmers, there was a way out. Provided that the owners of four-fifths of the land agreed, it was possible to get a special act of Parliament passed, by which all the land of the village, including the pasture, was divided up among the landowners so that each man's share was put all in one piece. By getting all the rich farmers to agree to do this, the new Squire was able to get the support of the owners of four-fifths of the land. Some poorer farmers, like William, did not want their land enclosed, but times had been hard and there were not many of them, for some had sold out to their richer neighbours. As a result they could do nothing to stop it. Now, in the late summer, a notice had been formally given out in church three times that it was proposed to apply to Parliament for an act to enclose the open fields and pastures of the village. To William it seemed the beginning of the end.

For a long time nothing much happened. The village was full of rumours and stories. Apparently it took some time to draw up and pass an act of Parliament, so long that some people began to think it might never happen. But then, one day in the summer of 1781 they at last heard that the act had been passed. Then things began to happen quite quickly. First came the surveyors, strangers, with tapes and chains and maps. Day after day they wandered about, marking, measuring and calculating, and plotted their results on an enormous map of the whole village on which was marked every single square foot of land and who owned it. Then there were the Commissioners. They sat in the village inn

and questioned every landowner, including William. They wanted to know everything: which strips he owned, how many cattle and sheep he was allowed to keep on the common pasture, and how many he could put on the fallow field each year. From this information they worked out exactly what area his share of land ought to be. When they had done this for everybody, they set about dividing the land on the map into neat rectangular fields of the right size, so that each man had what he was entitled to. While they were doing this, the whole village was seething with excitement, with everyone trying to guess where his land would be.

Effects of enclosure

At last the work was finished, and the map was open for inspection. With the rest of the villagers, William went to look at it. He found his little parcel of land was quite a distance out of the village, at a place where the soil was not very good. All the best land seemed to have gone to the Squire and his friends. William was in despair. All that he had now was about twelve acres of poor land nowhere near his cottage. But what was worse, he had to pay his share of the expense of drawing up and passing the enclosure act, of surveying and mapping the land and of dividing it up. In addition, he had to pay towards making the new roads which replaced the wandering field paths. He added up the cost of all this and it came to more than he could afford.

Fragment of the enclosure map for Stathern, Leicestershire. *Left:* the village; the orchards and small plots round it are left untouched. The land along the bottom is pasture. The rest of the land used to be divided into furlongs and strips. Each furlong is named, e.g. Upper Furlong. Every strip is numbered, and an index exists naming the owner. The Commissioners have drawn, in heavy black lines, the boundaries of the new fields and have put the names of their owners in large print, e.g. Yalding. The dots along the boundaries show who is responsible for hedging the field. All the pasture on this section went to the Duke of Rutland.

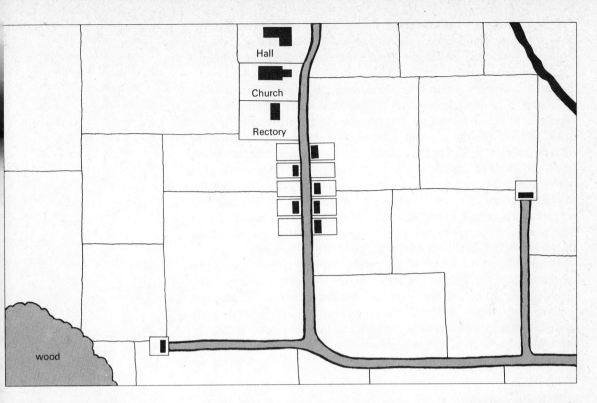

A village after enclosure. The land has now been divided up, and already two farmers have built new farm houses away from the village.

His son, John, refused to be so downcast. He pointed out that the nearby city of Nottingham was growing at an enormous pace, providing an expanding market for food. In addition the local gentry had got together to form a turnpike trust which was busy improving the road to the city. John was certain that there was a good living to be made by a small farmer growing produce and selling it in Nottingham. William took a lot of persuading but in the end he gave way. Anything was better than selling up. So he and his family got to work. They borrowed enough money to pay the expenses of enclosure and buy a horse and cart. They reared hens, kept a couple of cows and grew vegetables. Twice a week they went to Nottingham and sold their produce. It was hard work, and for a few years they only just kept their heads above water but in the end William was, if anything, better off than he had been before the great enclosure.

Some people were worse off than William. These were the cottagers who had no strips in the open fields, but had kept a few animals on the pasture. Everyone had taken it for granted that they had had a legal right to do this, but the Commissioners said it was just a custom, and they had no grazing rights. In consequence, when the land was shared out, they got nothing at all.

To begin with there was plenty of work for them fencing, ditching and draining the new fields and making the new roads. Even when all this had been done, some of them still found work cultivating the new crops which needed more labour than the old, especially as those farmers who tried using machines found them cumbersome, easily broken and difficult to repair. But the population of the village was growing so fast that some left and went to find jobs in the towns, while others has to be supported out of the parish rates.

The rich farmers, on the other hand, did well. A few of them found it necessary to borrow some money to pay their share of the enclosure expenses, set themselves up with machinery, get their land in good order and buy in the new fat animals, but within a year or so the increased production from their land more than paid for this. What was more the value of their land went up too, in some cases as much as tenfold. Soon Mr Jackson had built a fine new house, well away from the centre of the village, but right in the middle of his new estate. The other farmers soon followed his example and were very proud of their new homes. Some of them began to give themselves airs and make themselves rather ridiculous by trying to live like the gentry.

Meanwhile, in the centre of the village, there were only one or two farm buildings left. People who had been close neighbours now lived a mile or more apart. But they certainly became richer. Using the new methods they found their wheat crop increased fourfold, while their cattle and sheep weighed three times what they had done before. In the meantime the new hedges were growing apace, dividing the roads from the fields and one field from another. William could never get

A farmhouse, typical of those built by rich farmers at the end of the eighteenth century.

With their new wealth, the farmers found more time and money for hunting. They often found the new hedges tiresome.

used to these hedges, which cut him off from land where he had always wandered as he pleased. Nor could he get used to the strange emptiness of the village centre or to the fact that the village street now ended abruptly at a gate at each end, becoming simply a private road to a farm. The only public roads were the ones which led off at right-angles to the next villages. It seemed to William that, when the land was enclosed, something in the village had died. Certainly he was sure it would never be the same again.

What happened in William's village was in many ways typical. All over the Midlands the old open fields were being divided up into neat blocks of land. It used to be thought that these enclosures only really benefited the rich farmers. Certainly some people at the time complained that small farmers were forced out of business and labourers put out of work. We know now that this was not normally so. Official records show that there were usually just as many small farmers and labourers after enclosures as before. It is true that people were leaving villages and going to towns, but this was because the population was rising and not because the demand for labour on farms was falling. It was only where the land-owners turned all their land over to corn crops that the labourers found themselves with less to do. The country at large could not have done without the huge increase in the quality and quantity of food produced, for the population was growing rapidly. Thanks to the changes in the eighteenth century, the supply of food was able to keep pace with it. Here are some

extracts showing what people at the time thought about enclosure and their effect on people's lives.

First, two descriptions of the old system:

I found beans hidden among mustard growing wild as a weed: peas choked by poppies and corn-marigolds; every stem of barley fettered with convolvulus; wheat pining in thickets of couch and thistle.

The broadcast sowing had been performed in a most careless manner. Some parts seemed to have had the seed flung along them with a shovel while other parts contained only here and there a blade. This is shocking husbandry.

Now a description of an enclosed field.

I look over a large and level field of rich land, in which the drilled wheat is finely come up, and which is surrounded by clipped quickset hedges with a row of apple trees by the sides of them.

And now the poor.

The poor in these parishes may say with truth 'Parliament may be tender of property, all I know is I had a cow and an Act of Parliament has taken it from me'.

Now see what William Cobbett had to say about the state of labourers after enclosure in a corn-growing area.

The labourers' houses are beggarly in the extreme. The men and boys with dirty faces and dirty smock coats and dirty shirts. Invariably have I observed that the richer the soil, the more purely a corn country, the more miserable the labourers. The cause is this, the great, the big bull frog grasps all. Every inch of land is appropriated by the rich, and the wretched labourer has not a stick of wood and has no place for a pig or cow to graze, or even to lie down upon. Here, the horses plough the ground; they sow the ground, they hoe the

A clergyman is seen distributing charity to the poor women of the parish. In this case, at Durham, they received clay pipes and bundles of food.

166

A budget for one labouring family in the late eighteenth century was as follows: after paying for rent, clothes and furniture, the man had 7s. 3¾d. a week for himself, his wife and four children. This is how it was spent:

	s.	d.
Flour	4	10½
Yeast and salt		3
Tea, sugar and butter	1	0
Soap and blue		3¾
Candles		3
Potatoes		6
Thread and cloth		1½

This chart shows how much was spent in different ways on enclosures in the Sheffield area.

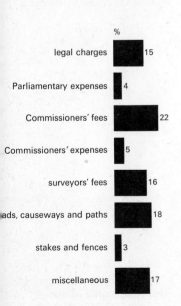

	%
legal charges	15
Parliamentary expenses	4
Commissioners' fees	22
Commissioners' expenses	5
surveyors' fees	16
ads, causeways and paths	18
stakes and fences	3
miscellaneous	17

ground; they carry the corn home; they thresh it out, and they carry it to market: nay, they rake the ground; they rake up the straggling straws and ears; so that they do the whole except the reaping and sowing. It is impossible to have an idea of anything more miserable than the state of the labourer in this part of the country.

To have a closer look at the labourer's lot, see what one of his family looking back on his childhood has to say:

My father was a day labouring man, who worked for seven or eight shillings in the winter, and in the summer for nine shillings a week, which is but a small pittance to keep a family. My mother bore eleven children, of which number I am the tenth. My parents being very poor, and receiving no support from the parish, we children fared very hard, and indeed seldom knew what it was to have a bellyful of victuals above once in the week. Suffering with hunger, cold and almost nakedness so embittered my life in my childhood, that I often wished secretly that I had been a brute, for then I could have filled my belly in the fields.

Finally, an unexpected result of enclosure.

Before the Commons were taken in, the children of the poor had ample space to recreate themselves at cricket, nurr and any other diversions; but now they are driven from every green spot and, in Bromsgrove here, the nailor boys, from force of circumstance, have taken possession of the turnpike road to play the before mentioned games, to the serious inconvenience of the passengers.

Things to do

1 Go through the extracts above carefully, and then make a list of the advantages and disadvantages of enclosures given by the writers quoted.
2 Study the budget of the eighteenth-century farm labourer given. What foods which we take for granted are missing from it?
3 Find out if the land in your area was enclosed in the eighteenth century. If it was, the local County Record Office may have the map drawn up by the Commissioners, and may be able to supply a photographic copy for study.
4 This account was written from the point of view of a poor farmer. Try writing one from the point of view of one of his rich neighbours.
5 Find out what 'nurr' is, and find out what other games were played in the country in the eighteenth century.

Books to read

J. Addy, *The Agrarian Revolution*, Longmans
V. Skipp, *An Eighteenth-Century Farm Labourer's Family*, Oxford University Press
B. Taylor, *Robert Bakewell*, Macmillan

Chapter 13
The Industrial Revolution

Industry as it used to be

The Lord Chancellor, who is chairman of the House of Lords, sits on a woolsack. This is not because a sack of wool is the most comfortable possible seat, but because in the Middle Ages when the custom began, the prosperity of the country depended on the production and sale of wool. Many men made fortunes from it, but, on the other hand, whole villages were sometimes swept away to make room for more sheep, and thus bring more profit to the landowner. Later, though the wool trade ceased to be the most profitable, the actual manufacture of cloth remained the most important single industry in the country. Not that only woollen cloth was produced. Since 1640 ships belonging to the East India Company had been bringing cotton from India and cotton working was quite an important industry in Lancashire.

Now today industry means towns and factories, vast organizations with enormous capital and huge machines with tremendous power. Three hundred years ago it meant none of these. The cloth industry was carried on in quiet country villages by people working in their own homes on simple spinning wheels and hand looms which relied for their power on the muscles of the men and women who worked them. There was no question of going out to work, of clocking in or payment by the hour. The weaver was paid for each piece of cloth he produced and, to earn a decent wage – ten shillings per week – he had to work for more than fourteen hours a day. If this seems a lot of work for only a little money, you must remember that the weaver had his family to help him in his work, and that his pay was more than that of a farm labourer. Working indoors, with his family around him, his wife spinning, his son helping on his loom, the hand-loom weaver at the beginning of the eighteenth century was not badly off.

Spinners at work. Spinning requires little strength, and was usually done by women.

Down with cotton!

But a revolution was at hand in the cotton industry. For years the wool manufacturers had been trying to get rid of the competition of cotton, which was becoming more popular year by year. At last, in 1721, they persuaded Parliament to pass an act forbidding the importation of finished cotton cloth. But this did them little good, for all that happened was that the importation of raw cotton increased enormously. The only difficulty for the cotton merchants was that all this cotton had to be processed, and the number of spinners and weavers available could not easily be increased – and neither could their hours of work! Some means had to be found whereby a man could produce more

Left: a hand loom. The weaver holds the shuttle in his left hand. *Right:* the thread is wound from the spindles on to a large frame.

finished cloth in the same amount of time. It was a difficult problem, but there were men at hand with the intelligence and the determination to solve it.

The Flying Shuttle 1733

The first of these men was John Kay, born in Lancashire in 1704. He was the son of a wealthy clothier and in 1733 he was living in Colchester supervising weavers, who were working for his father. In weaving, one lot of threads, called the warp, is stretched out on the loom, and the cloth is made by passing another thread, the woof, through at right-angles to it. The woof is carried on a shuttle which, at the beginning of the eighteenth century, was threaded through the warp by hand. On small machines, this was done by the weaver himself leaning across the front of his loom, but on bigger looms two men had to work, one on each side, passing the shuttle from one to the other. This was a slow process, and, to speed it up, Kay devised a 'Flying Shuttle', which the weaver could send 'flying' from one side of the loom to the other simply by pulling a string. This invention made work easier and quicker for all weavers and made it possible for big looms to be operated by only one man.

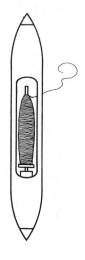

Kay's flying shuttle.

Kay was very proud of his invention but, to his amazement, the Colchester weavers refused to use it. They feared that the new shuttle would put some of them out of work and forced Kay to leave the town. He went to Leeds, where to his relief, he found weavers who were prepared to give his invention a try. It was a success and the weavers found their work easier and their output greater. All was well until Kay tried to get them to pay him for his invention. They refused. Kay took them to court, and eventually won his case. The weavers still refused to pay and, his spirit broken, Kay returned to his native town of Bury to retire. Meanwhile, his invention was taken up all over the north of England and the weavers began to use thread more quickly than the spinners could produce it. Kay could not resist the challenge, and set to work to try to improve the traditional spinning wheel. The Bury spinners heard what he was about and feared that they might be put out of work. They therefore broke into his house and smashed everything that they could lay their hands on. Kay himself only escaped with his life because two friends carried him out hidden in a roll of cloth. He had had enough and left Britain for good. It was Britain's loss. 'I have a great many more inventions that I have given in,' he wrote to a friend, 'and the reason I have not put them forward is the bad treatment I have had.' Ten years later he died in France, in great poverty.

The Spinning Jenny 1768

Fortunately, there were others to carry on Kay's work. One of these was James Hargreaves, a working weaver of Blackburn, who succeeded in inventing a spinning machine. This machine, which he called a

A replica of Hargreaves' Spinning Jenny. It was worked by turning the handle at the side.

'Jenny' after his wife, could spin eight threads at once. Later improvements increased this number to 120. Hargreaves learned from Kay's experiences, and kept his invention a secret, using it only to produce thread for his own loom. But his neighbours' suspicions were aroused by the strange noises coming from Hargreaves' home. When he sold a few machines to buy food for his family, in 1768, the mob broke in and smashed his Jenny to matchwood. Hargreaves left Lancashire and settled at Nottingham where he patented the machine and started a small business which kept him in comfort until his death in 1778. Meanwhile, many spinners adopted his Jenny, in spite of the rather thin weak thread it spun.

The Water Frame   1769

While Hargreaves had been at work on his Spinning Jenny, another inventor, Richard Arkwright, had been thinking about the same problem. Arkwright was a very extraordinary man. He was born at Preston in 1732, the youngest of a family of thirteen. He had no education to speak of, and began life as a barber's apprentice. At the age of eighteen he set up in business on his own at Bolton, but soon lost interest in barbering, which did not pay very well, and began to turn over in his mind the problems of inventing a spinning machine. With the help of a clock-maker, he set to work and produced some working models. Meanwhile his business was going to rack and ruin and his wife, fearing that her husband's neglect of his trade would reduce the whole family to starvation, smashed all his models in an attempt to bring him to his senses. The only result was a violent quarrel which led to their separation. The work on a spinning machine went on. Finally Arkwright succeeded in building the first satisfactory working model in the house of the headmaster of Preston Grammar School. But rumours were circulating. Two old women, hearing the machine humming, even accused Arkwright of raising the Devil, whose bagpipes they thought they had heard playing. Then, hearing how Hargreaves' Jenny had been smashed at Blackburn, the inventor decided to run no further risk and moved to Nottingham, where he found two manufacturers to finance his experiments.

By 1769 his work was far enough advanced for him to take out a patent and put his machine on the market. He called it the 'Spinning Frame' and the threads it produced were stronger than those made by the Jenny. But, most important, it needed too much power to be worked by hand. The earliest models were powered by horses, but in 1771 Arkwright built a spinning mill in which the power was provided by a water wheel. From this time on, spinning moved out of the house. As the thread produced by the new machine was stronger and cheaper than that made by the spinning wheel, more and more spinners gave up their wheels and went to work in the mills. Arkwright began to make money. Of course he had his troubles. In 1779 his own workers

Above: Arkwright's original spinning frame, made in 1769.

Left: by 1775 Arkwright's machine had been modified to look like this.

destroyed his mill at Chorley, but he simply built another in Scotland, where the workers were more co-operative. 'Whoever loses, it won't be me,' he said grimly. He was right. By working at least sixteen hours a day he more than kept his head above water, and in 1786 he was knighted. He died in 1792, worn out by years of incessant work, but worth a lot of money.

The Mule

Before his death, Arkwright's water frame was superseded by an invention which combined his ideas with those of Hargreaves. This clever device, which could spin a thread finer than had ever been spun before, was the work of a shy and retiring Bolton spinner named Samuel Crompton. He built his machine, called the 'Mule', simply to use himself so that he could make more money by selling his super-fine thread. But as soon as this appeared on the market, questions were asked and the unfortunate man was given no peace until he promised to share his secret with the local manufacturers. Trusting to their promises of vast wealth, he gave them all the details and received, in return, less than £100. For years he waited patiently for his reward until someone took up his case in Parliament. Then, in 1812, when his invention was giving work to 70,000 spinners, he was voted £5,000, which he invested in a business which went bankrupt. He eventually died in 1827, no better off for his inventions.

Crompton's mule: a very complicated machine.

The impossible machine

These inventions in the spinning industry had by 1790 solved the problem of supplying the weavers. Indeed, it was now impossible for the hand looms to use all the thread the spinners were producing. As early as 1784 the problem of how to speed up weaving had been worrying clothiers and a group of them were discussing it at Matlock in the presence of a mild and scholarly clergyman, named Edmund Cartwright. Cartwright, who was forty-one years old, had just been round one of Arkwright's mills, and suggested that to solve the difficulty Arkwright should invent a weaving machine. He was at once howled down by his friends, who assured him that the process was much too complicated for a machine ever to do it. Cartwright, who had never seen a loom working in his life, decided to prove them wrong and went back to his rectory in Leicestershire. Here he proceeded, with the help of the local smith and carpenter, to build a working power loom, which he at once patented. He now gave up his parish and moved to Doncaster, where he set up a small mill, where his machines were powered by a bull. In 1791 a Manchester firm set up a few of his looms in a mill and found that the weavers' output doubled. Delighted, they at once halved the rates of pay. The weavers, furious, burned the whole mill down to the ground. Frightened by this experience, other mill-owners hesitated to use Cartwright's machines, and the unfortunate inventor found himself bankrupt. Gradually, however, power looms began to come into their own and by 1813 there were 2,400 of them. Nor was the inventor forgotten, for Parliament voted him £10,000 and he was able to spend his last years on a farm in Kent, amusing himself by inventing agricultural machinery.

The new cloth industry

Cartwright's invention of the power loom made the revolution in the cloth industry complete. In place of the quiet country villages with their hand looms and spinning wheels, there were now huge mills crowded with machines getting their power from a single shaft running the length of the building. The spinners and weavers were now no more than machine minders and many of the older ones found it difficult to adjust to the change. Nimble hands were needed, and small bodies could more easily slip in between the machines. In addition, with the use of power, physical strength was no longer required. The answer was obvious and more and more children were employed in these new mills. They worked for less money, and soon the wages of a weaver working sixteen hours a day for six days a week were as low as nine shillings a week, while food prices were rising. As he worked away in the mill, before going to his house, one of many built by the mill-owner as cheaply as possible, and therefore uncomfortable and insanitary, the unfortunate weaver might well have wished that the machine breakers had done a more thorough job.

On the other hand, the new inventions did bring about an enormous

The interior of a cloth mill, engraved about 1840. Notice the child crawling about under the machinery, and the wretched clothing of the workers. The owner stands in the background.

increase in the production of cheap cloth, which meant that Britons were better clothed than ever before. In addition, vast quantities of cloth were exported, which increased the wealth of the country. The trouble was that the increased wealth was badly distributed: too much went to the mill-owners and too little to the mill-workers. It was to be many years before the balance was redressed. In the meantime, if the worker wanted to improve his lot, he had to be prepared to fight to do it.

Power for the mills

The great need of the new mills was power. Water power was cheap, but to use it, the mill had to be built alongside a stream. What was more it was unreliable. A long period of drought might result in the stream drying up, and the mill had to close down until it rained. Other sources of power had to be found. Now some mills were using steam pumps to raise water into their mill reservoirs, but these pump engines could not be adapted to drive machinery. They had been invented in 1712 by Thomas Newcomen, a Devon man, and really worked by air

This engraving of Newcomen's engine dates from 1717. The figure of a man (*left*) gives an idea of the size of the engine.

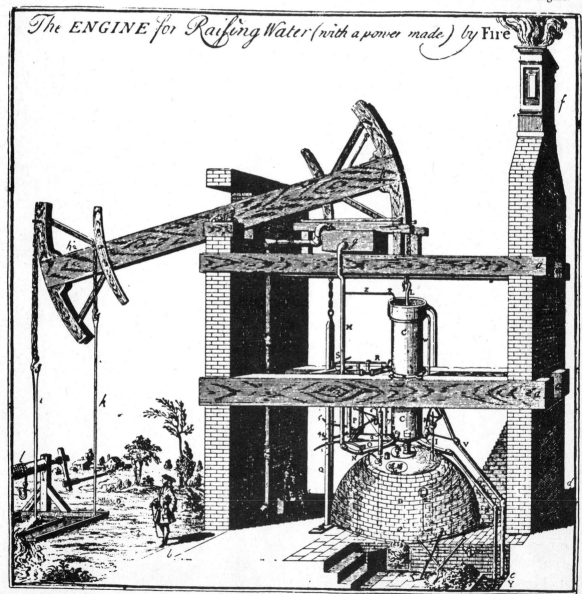

pressure. The engine consisted of a huge beam, pivoted in the middle, with a piston and cylinder on the one end, and a pump at the other. The pump was heavier than the piston, and thus pulled it to the top of the cylinder. At this point the cylinder was filled with steam from a boiler, and then suddenly cooled. The steam at once condensed and created a vacuum. The pressure of air on the top of the cylinder pushed the piston to the bottom and pulled the pump to the top. Steam was then let into the cylinder again, the piston went back up to the top, and the process began again.

This engine had several disadvantages, but the main one was that the cylinder had to be heated up and cooled down at every working stroke, and it was reckoned that four-fifths of the steam was used in heating the cylinder, and only one-fifth in filling it. A young Scot named James Watt, employed at Glasgow University, repairing their model engines, was sent a Newcomen engine to put right. He fell to wondering if its design could not be improved to make it more efficient. In 1765, he thought of the answer – a separate condensation chamber connected to the cylinder by a valve. He tried it out on a model and it worked, but the first full-size engine was spoiled by bad workmanship. It was not until 1775 that things began to improve, for it was then that Watt went into partnership with Matthew Boulton, a Birmingham businessman and manufacturer with a skilled labour force. Soon Watt managed to produce an engine in which the steam actually did the

Watt's rotative beam engine, 1797.

work. Next he made one in which the steam could be used to push the piston both ways along the cylinder and this, coupled with a crank mechanism, made it possible for this engine to drive machinery. By 1800, when they retired, Boulton and Watt had set up about 500 engines, some in cotton mills, some in coalmines, some on canals and some in breweries. Watt had even had the idea of driving wagons by steam, but had never followed it up. As Boulton said to George III, he and Watt sold 'what all the world desires – power'. Once again these inventions resulted in a great increase in production and wealth. Once again the increase was badly distributed.

The ironmasters

To make these engines, large quantities of iron were needed. The iron industry was, of course, a very ancient one indeed. For centuries past iron ore had been dug from the ground and smelted into iron with charcoal. This process used vast quantities of wood so that the industry had to be carried on in forest areas. By the beginning of the seventeenth century, there was serious concern lest all the forests might be destroyed. If only some other fuel could be found, all might be well. In 1620 Lord Dudley seemed to have found the answer, for he took out a patent for smelting iron using coal. This new process was in fact the work of his illegitimate son, Dud Dudley, who was only twenty-one. Like most inventors, he found that his discoveries upset many of his

Charcoal burning was far from easy. To make charcoal, the wood has to smoulder but not burst into flames. This was usually achieved by covering the fire with turves to exclude most of the air.

fellow-workers. He made iron by the new method at Cradley, but was attacked by the local charcoal-burners and was finally flooded out by a rainstorm. Not a whit dismayed, he built another furnace near Sedgeley, which was soon turning out seven tons of iron a week. But he was not to be left in peace. The timber-fellers, charcoal-burners and blacksmiths all ganged up and destroyed his furnace again. This time Dud was in serious trouble, for he had had to borrow money to build his furnace at Sedgeley and now could not pay it back. As a result he was put into a debtors' prison, from which he was released just before the Civil War. He spent the war organizing arms production for the King, which did him no good when the King lost. After the Restoration he tried to re-establish himself in industry, but failed. His discovery was forgotten, and when he died in 1684, the forests were still being destroyed to provide charcoal to smelt iron.

One of the centres of the iron industry was in the West Midlands, and, in the eighteenth century, one of the most important works was at Coalbrookdale in Shropshire. These works were owned by the Darby family, who were Quakers. Abraham Darby, who had bought the works in 1708, followed on where Dud Dudley had left off, and in 1709 began to use coke to smelt iron and was soon using nothing else. Throughout the eighteenth century the works grew, making engines, pumps and rails and it is still in production today. The greatest monument to the Darby family and to their faith in iron is, however,

Blast furnaces of an iron foundry. In the foreground are cakes of metal.

the great iron bridge spanning the Severn near Coalbrookdale. This bridge was cast at Coalbrookdale and erected by Abraham Darby III in 1779. It was the first iron bridge in the world, and it still stands today.

Iron-mad Wilkinson

Other ironmasters, too, made important discoveries. John Wilkinson, of Bilston in Staffordshire, invented a machine for boring cylinders for James Watt, and used one of Watt's steam engines to blow his blast furnaces at a time when most other iron-makers were using water power. He could see no limits to the uses to which iron might be put. He built an iron ship, had an iron lavatory, and even kept an iron coffin in which he hoped to be buried. It was no wonder that he was called 'Iron-mad Wilkinson'. Through the efforts of men like these Midland ironmasters, the production of iron increased enormously during the eighteenth century and the quality of the metal was greatly improved. Thus, when Britain went to war with France in 1793, there was no shortage of ironworks in which to make the necessary guns and ammunition. But they were no longer to be found in the forests. Instead they moved to the coalfields of the Midlands and north, where there was plenty of the new fuel to fire the furnaces.

Black diamonds

On the coalfields, too, there were changes. Most of the coal produced in 1700 was for ordinary domestic use, and the pits were very shallow. The coal was only worked close to the bottom of the shaft because of the difficulty of ventilating the mine, and the workings often filled with water. As the century went on, the demand for coal increased, so deeper shafts were sunk and longer passages were tunnelled out under the ground. The problem of flooding was solved by using the improved steam pumping engines, but there still remained the problems of ventilating and lighting the pit. Sometimes they tried sinking two shafts and then lighting a fire at the bottom of one of them to make the air circulate. The trouble was that this led to dreadful explosions when the gases in the mine were drawn into the fire.

These gases also made almost any form of light in the mine dangerous, yet the miners could not work in darkness. No really satisfactory miners' lamp was invented in the eighteenth century, and the miners used to take caged birds down the mine with them, because they had found that the gas affected the birds before it was concentrated enough to explode. Thus, when the bird died, they still had enough time to get out before the gas would explode. In other mines, before work was started, a man was sent down carrying a long pole, with a light at the end. Wrapped in wet clothes, he crawled alone through the dark mine pushing the pole before him, combing the air with its flame. When he found a pocket of gas, the flame ignited it, and there was a small explosion. If he was fortunate, the pole was long enough

Wilkinson token (see page 191).

Above left: the iron bridge near Coalbrookdale. Its designer, Thomas Pritchard, made it the same shape as a traditional stone or brick bridge.

Below left: Coalbrookdale at night, with the furnaces lighting the sky, and the work still going on.

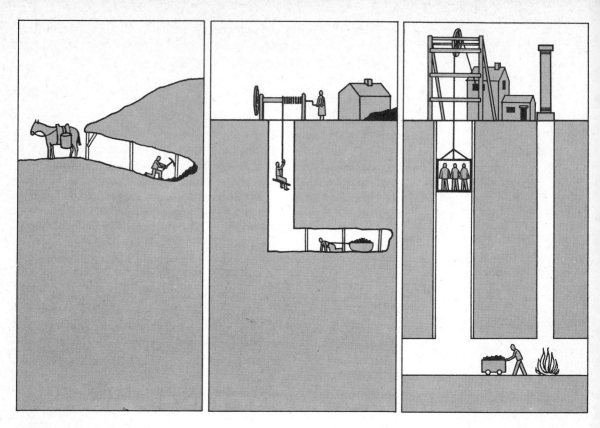

to keep his crouching body from harm and he could go on his way, clearing the air for his fellow-miners who followed him down at a safe distance. Yet in spite of such precautions explosions were all too common, and the increased quantities of coal were only mined at an enormous cost in men's lives.

Eighteenth-century roads

The great revolution in industry led to a huge transport problem. New materials had to be brought to the mills and factories and the finished goods had to be taken away to be sold. Eighteenth-century roads just could not cope. The real trouble was that nobody had really thought how to make a road which could stand up to any weight of traffic. Some new roads had been built, mainly in Scotland, but these were military roads, and did not have to carry huge wagons with wheels more than a foot wide and so heavily loaded that eight horses could barely move them. Nor did they have to cope with strings of packhorses jostling with heavy coaches and herds of cattle and sheep. In fact the only method of road construction used was to dig out a ditch on each side of the road, and throw the soil from them into the middle in the hope that the traffic would flatten it into a smooth surface. In fact, it broke it up into ruts and mud. But let some travellers speak for

Three stages in coal-mining. *Left:* an early mine, near the surface. *Centre:* when surface coal had been worked out, deeper shafts were sunk. The gallery is too low for a man to stand upright. *Right:* a mine with two shafts, about 700 ft deep. The lift is run by a power-driven cable.

themselves. First, here is what Daniel Defoe, author of *Robinson Crusoe*, wrote about a stretch of main road in the Midlands.

This road is not passable but just in the middle of summer, after the Coal Carriages have beaten the way; for as the ground is a stiff clay, so, after rain, the water stands as in a dish, and horses sink in it up to their bellies.

Arthur Young, the Farmers' friend, was even more insulting about a road in Essex. 'It is,' he wrote,

for near twelve miles so narrow that a mouse cannot pass by any carriage. I must not forget the eternally meeting with chalk wagons, stuck fast, till a collection of them are in the same situation and twenty or thirty horses may be tacked to each to draw them out one by one.

So much for the Midlands and east, but it was the same story everywhere. One traveller described the roads of Monmouthshire as 'mere ditches', while Arthur Young warned travellers to avoid a road in the north

as they would the Devil; for a thousand to one they break their necks or their limbs by overthrows or breakings down. They will here meet with ruts, which I actually measured four feet deep, and floating with mud only from a wet summer. The only mending it receives is tumbling in some loose stones, which serve no other purpose than jolting a carriage in a most intolerable manner.

Malachy Postlethwayt, writing in 1774, described a Sussex road

sixty to a hundred yards broad, lying from side to side all poached with cattle, yet no going with a horse, but at every step up to the shoulders, full of sloughs and holes and covered with standing water.

All kinds of livestock, even turkeys and geese, were driven to Smithfield Market, London by drovers. These drove roads were old-established tracks which other traffic avoided because of the bad surface caused by the continual passage of cattle.

Perhaps not all roads were quite as bad as this. Angry travellers are always inclined to exaggerate, but some idea of their general condition can be gained from the fact that it took a coach in 1760 sixteen days to travel the 400 miles between London and Edinburgh in good weather. Clearly something had to be done. Since 1555, it had been the responsibility of each parish to keep its roads in good repair and all its citizens were meant to work for six days a year on the roads. In fact, they did little, treating the six days as a sort of picnic. By 1700 the government had recognized that this system did not work, and tried another. They set up 'Turnpike Trusts', responsible for repairing the roads, and gave them permission to levy tolls on the road users to get their money back. These tolls were collected at gates, or turnpikes, at intervals along the road. Foot passengers were exempt from payment, as were soldiers and Royal Mail coaches. These coaches used to warn the gate-keepers of their approach by sounding their posthorns so that the gates could be opened to let them through. Though the gates have vanished, many of the old toll-houses still stand at the roadside.

Tolls to be taken at
LLANFAIR GATE

s.d

For every Horse, Mule, or other Cattle, drawing any Coach or other Carriage, with springs the sum of 4

For every Horse, Mule or other Beast or Cattle drawing any Waggon Cart or other such Carriage not employed solely in carrying or going empty to fetch Lime for manure the sum of 3

For every Horse, Mule, or other Beast or Cattle, drawing any Waggon, Cart, or other such Carriage, employed solely in carrying or going empty to fetch Lime for manure the sum of 1

For every Horse, Mule, or Ass, laden or unladen, and not drawing, the sum of 1

For every Drove of Oxen, Cows, or other neat Cattle per score, the sum of 10

For every Drove of Calves, Sheep, Lambs, or Pigs per score, the sum of 5

For every Horse, Mule or other Beast drawing any Waggon, or Cart, the Wheels being less than 3 inches in breadth, or having Wheels with Tires fastened with Nails projecting and not countersunk to pay double Toll.

A Ticket taken here clears Carnedd Du Bar.

Now from the very start, these tollgates were very unpopular, and were often attacked and destroyed by mobs. In 1734 Parliament even imposed the death penalty for destroying tollgates to try to stop these attacks, but in 1749 anti-turnpike riots at Bristol lasted for a fortnight, and were only suppressed by bringing in six troops of dragoons! There was good reason for their unpopularity. A few of the trusts made enormous profits, but many of them were deeply in debt through bad management. What was worse, they did not really improve the roads. 'The wagoners,' wrote one observer,

say that whereas they had been told that, by paying a little money for a few years, they should have roads so good as to be able to carry greater loads, and use fewer horses, they now find the roads are so much worse that they are oblig'd to add an horse or two, instead of taking any off, and still pay the same money, yet do not know when this expense will end.

The Tottenham Court Road Tollgate. The scale of charges is on the left, behind the gatekeeper's office. Next to the office is a narrow gate for horsemen, and then two carriage gates. Posts are set to allow pedestrians to pass, but not carriages. The fat man seems in some difficulty.

Blind Jack

When, in 1765, the first really good roads were engineered, it was done by a man who had not seen a road since he was six – Blind Jack Metcalf of Knaresborough. In spite of being blinded by smallpox, he was a great walker, and knew the country so well that he used to guide people across the moors. In 1765 he heard that a new turnpike road was to be built from Harrogate to Boroughbridge and got a contract to make three miles of it. His road was carefully laid, with a foundation of large, jagged stones, covered with smaller stones and gravel, arched so that it would drain into a large ditch on each side. So successful was this piece of road, that Blind Jack was given other contracts amounting in all to almost 200 miles of road for various trusts in the north. He made over £50,000, and died in 1810 at the age of ninety-three, leaving behind him roads which would carry any weight of traffic without breaking up into ruts and potholes.

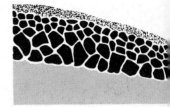

Road surfaces (1) Blind Jack Metcalf.

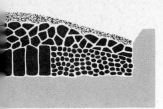

(2) Telford.

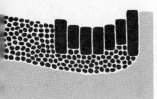

(3) Macadam.

The Scottish roadbuilders

Metcalf's work was carried on by Thomas Telford, a Scotsman from Dumfries. He began work as a mason, building bridges, and went on from that to road-making. His earliest work was done in the Highlands of Scotland, where he made 920 miles of road, and built over 1,000 bridges. His roads, like Metcalf's, were made by putting small stones on a foundation of large ones, only he used flat stones instead of jagged ones in the foundation. His roads wore well, and his fame spread. Finally, in 1810, he was asked by the Postmaster-General to survey the London–Holyhead road. In 1815, he began work, using money voted by Parliament. By 1830 he had completed a road nearly 300 miles long and thirty feet wide. In its day it was the finest road in Britain. The marvel of it is the great suspension bridge built at the cost of £120,000 to carry the road over the Menai straits into Anglesey.

Metcalf's and Telford's methods were copied by Turnpike Trusts all over the country, and roads improved. But they were expensive to make, and a Scotsman named John Macadam, who worked for a trust near Bristol, eventually devised a much cheaper method of road-making which proved just as good. He used no foundation of large stones, but simply laid a ten-inch layer of stones, none of them more than an inch in diameter, straight on to the subsoil. He mostly used limestone or sandstone, which slowly ground away to fill every crack and space with powder. This powder acted as a sort of cement to bind the surface together and turn the water. Soon, Macadam became famous, and his method of road-making was adopted all over the country. The result was that by 1820 the country was covered with a network of fine coaching roads, able to bear any weight of traffic. The journey from London to Edinburgh, which had taken sixteen days in 1750 took only forty hours in 1830. Here is how Dickens described a coach journey over the new roads in *Pickwick Papers*.

The wheels skim over the hard and frosty ground: and the horses, bursting into a canter at a smart crack of the whip, step along the road as if the load behind them: coach, passengers, cod fish, oyster barrels, and all: were but a feather at their heels. They have descended a gentle slope, and enter upon a level as compact and dry as a solid block of marble, two miles long. Another crack of the whip, and on they speed at a smart gallop: the horses tossing their heads and rattling the harness, as if in exhilaration at the rapidity of the motion.

Contrast this with an eighteenth-century traveller's experience:

I had a very bad journey into Buckinghamshire, and like to have been overturned twenty times. The passengers alighted several times, up to the mid legs in dirt, and walked for miles in dirty, splashy ways.

Clearly, travellers had much to thank Blind Jack and his fellow road-makers for.

Artificial rivers

But this improvement in roads had been too slow, and another method of transport had been developed. Rivers, especially the Severn, the Trent, the Thames and the Yorkshire Ouse, had always been important highways, and various people had played with the idea of linking them together with artificial rivers, or canals. The man who more than anyone else made this idea a reality was James Brindley, born in 1716, the son of a farmer. He received no education before being apprenticed to a wheelwright, but had a wonderful knack of at once seeing the solution to problems in engineering which the engineers themselves had given up in despair. In this way he made quite a reputation for himself, and thus came his great chance. In 1759, the Duke of Bridgewater got permission from Parliament to make a canal to carry coal from his mines at Worsley to Manchester – a distance of seven miles. By road the cartage charge for this distance was nine shillings a ton, and the Duke thought this was too much and believed that it would be cheaper by water. He heard that Brindley was good at solving practical problems, and asked him to come to discuss the proposed canal. Jim was all confidence. He was quite sure he could do the job himself, and made what he called an 'ochilor servey' of the ground. He found that the biggest obstacle to cross was the valley of the River Irwell. The Duke took it for granted that the canal would go down one side of the valley and up the other in a series of locks, but Jim treated this idea with scorn. He proposed to carry the canal over the river by means of a bridge – a revolutionary idea. Rather dazed, the Duke agreed.

Soon, work started. Brindley had no detailed maps, and was quite unable to work anything out on paper. He had only a general idea of how his canal was to be built, and, if a difficulty arose, simply went to bed until he had solved it. He had plenty of labourers, many of them Irish, but they had only picks and shovels to move the tons of earth necessary to navigate a canal. In spite of all the difficulties, work went ahead. The great aqueduct over the Irwell was built, and in 1761 the canal was filled with water from end to end. What was more, the water stayed there. Brindley had assured everybody that a layer of kneaded or 'puddled' clay was all that was required to stop the water leaking out, but many had not believed him. Now he was proved right. The canal was a great success. Stage coaches were diverted so that the passengers could see the marvellous aqueduct and, more important, the price of coal in Manchester fell from sevenpence to threepence halfpenny a hundredweight.

This canal was only the beginning of Brindley's work. By 1767 he had built another to link Manchester with Runcorn and had worked out a plan to link the Thames, the Trent and the Mersey by a network of canals 260 miles long. By the time he died in 1772 much of this was complete, and the work was carried on after his death by others, among them Telford. These canals could carry huge loads very cheaply – at

The Irwell aqueduct.

about a quarter of the cost of road haulage – and still make a handsome profit. As a result, large numbers of canals were dug by small companies, and they often made their locks different sizes, or their canals different depths. This made it very difficult to make a boat which could be used on all the canals in the country, and cargoes often had to be transferred from one boat to another on a long journey. Some canal companies were inefficient, and gave a very poor service, while others tried to make canals too cheaply, only to find the banks washing away. Yet in spite of all this, it was only canals that made it possible for Britain to become an industrial country, for only they could carry the necessary weight of coal, iron, clay and cloth.

Woolsack or coalbag?

So much for the changes in Britain's industries and the men who helped to bring them about. They were changes which affected the whole character of the country. As a result of the inventions of the eighteenth century, Britain was able to produce good quality articles more cheaply than any other country of the day, and thus became 'The Workshop of the World'. This brought wealth and prosperity to the country, but too little of it went into the pockets of the ordinary workers. As the factories began to spring up where coal and iron were plentiful, towns to house the workers grew up around them, and were linked by roads and canals. These new roads and canals tended to draw

189

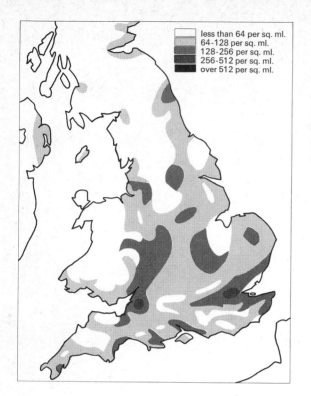

less than 64 per sq. ml.
64–128 per sq. ml.
128–256 per sq. ml.
256–512 per sq. ml.
over 512 per sq. ml.

more industry and more workers from the countryside into the towns. In fact, the balance of the whole population began to shift. Before 1750, the most densely populated part of the country was the south and east – the richest farming land. After 1800 it was in the north and west, on the coalfields. Indeed, in the nineteenth century the Lord Chancellor ought really to have changed his Woolsack for a bag of coal, but he never did.

Left: distribution of population in about 1700.
Right: distribution of population in about 1900. Apart from London, the highly populated areas all surround coalfields.

Dates to remember

1709   First smelting with coke by Abraham Darby
1733   Flying Shuttle invented by Kay
1761   Duke of Bridgewater's canal opened
1765   Metcalf began work in Yorkshire
1769   Arkwright's Water Frame patented
1775   Watt's first successful steam engine

Things to do

1   Try to find out which of the changes described in the chapter applied to your area. In particular, find out whether any new industries grew up in your district during the Industrial Revolution.

Also find out about local turnpike roads and look out for toll-houses. The County Record Office will have details.

2 Read the following extract, written by Richard Oastler, who lived in a little cloth town in Yorkshire. He was recalling how things had been in his youth. When you have read it, answer the questions below it.

It was the custom for the children at that time, to mix learning their trades with other instruction and with amusement, and they learned their trades or their occupations, not by being put into places, to stop there from morning to night, but by having a little work to do, and then some little time for instruction, and they were generally under the immediate care of their parents; the villages about Leeds and Huddersfield were occupied by respectable little clothiers, who could manufacture a piece of cloth or two in a week, or three or four or five pieces, and always had their family at home; and they could at that time make a good profit by what they sold; there were filial affection and parental feeling, and not over-labour; but that race of manufacturers has been almost completely destroyed; there are scarcely any of the old-fashioned domestic manufacturers left, and the villages are composed of one or two, or in some cases three or four mill-owners, and the rest, poor creatures who are reduced and ground down to want, and in general are compelled to live upon the labour of their little ones.

(a) Did Oastler think the Industrial Revolution a good or bad thing?

(b) What changes had he seen that led him to this opinion?

(c) What other changes were there that could be quoted on the other side of the argument?

3 Find out if any tokens were issued in your area, and what organization issued them.

Things to discuss

1 Taking the cloth industry as an example, what qualities were necessary for success in industry in the eighteenth century?

2 What, if anything, could have been done to make sure that the wealth created by the Industrial Revolution was more fairly shared out?

Books to read

M. E. Beggs-Humphreys, *The Industrial Revolution, 1760–1860*, Allen & Unwin

M. Blakeway, *A Canal Builder*, Oxford University Press

J. L. Davies (ed.), *James Watt and Steam Power*, Cape (Jackdaw)

M. Greenwood, *Roads and Canals in the Eighteenth Century*, Longmans

L. Meynell, *Thomas Telford*, Bodley Head

L. T. C. Rolt, *Inland Waterways*, Ward, Lock Educational

R. B. Sawrey-Cookson, *Roads*, Ward, Lock Educational

R. Whately, *An Eighteenth-Century Toll-Keeper*, Oxford University Press

N. Wymer, *James Watt*, Oxford University Press

There was a chronic shortage of copper coin in the eighteenth century, which led many factory owners to make their own with which to pay their workers. This Coalbrookdale ½d. token of 1792 shows an inclined plane at Ketley for elevating barges.

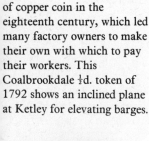

Chapter 14
Developments in science

Science in 1603

If you could travel back through time to 1603 and talk to a young schoolboy of about your own age, James Robinson, the mercer's son, you would find him a great puzzle. If, for instance, you were to ask him what he knew about science, he would not have understood what you meant. You would have had to explain that you wanted to know, for instance, in what way the sun and the planets revolved, or how various chemicals reacted on each other, what rules controlled the transmission of light and heat, or why things drop when you let them go. Or perhaps you might have been interested in how he would have divided up animals and plants into groups. Anyway, whatever you had asked, the answer would have surprised you.

For instance, he would probably have told you that the earth was the centre of the universe, and that all the other planets, the sun and the stars revolved round it. Indeed, he could probably have shown you a book with diagrams to show how it all worked. He might have heard that a Polish monk, named Copernicus, had said that this was not so; that the earth revolved round the sun, but he would have taken no notice of this revolutionary theory. Why should he believe the teaching of a solitary monk when it was opposed to that of all other scholars right back to the ancient Greeks? As for chemistry, he would have told you that everything was made from the four elements of fire, water, air and earth, and that there was no reason why a metal like lead could not be turned into gold. If you had told him that this was impossible, he would have pointed out that many very intelligent men were convinced that it could be done, and were devoting their lives to trying to do it. Such clever men would not waste their time trying to do the impossible.

By now you would begin to think that Jim was rather ignorant and stupid, and when you found out how little he knew about light, heat, gravity and biology, you would think him very ignorant indeed, especially when you remembered that he knew nothing about electricity, petrol engines, steam power, and probably believed in witches. But you would not have been making a very good impression either. If Jim heard that you had been to school ever since you were five, he would expect you to have a pretty good knowledge of Latin – enough to be able to read a book in Latin without any difficulty, and to have a sound knowledge of Greek and Roman literature. He would have thought this much more important than all this scientific nonsense. When he found out that you did not know these things, he would have been just as shocked at your ignorance as you were at his!

This diagram shows how ancient scientists thought the universe was arranged.

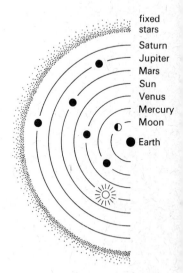

fixed stars
Saturn
Jupiter
Mars
Sun
Venus
Mercury
Moon
Earth

You would have felt much more at home if you could have come forward 180 years, and met Jim's descendant, William. True, William would have still known a lot more about Latin and Greek than you do, but on the other hand, he would have known much more about science, especially chemistry, physics and astronomy, than did Jim. In fact, he too would have marvelled at Jim's ignorance, for many vitally important discoveries had been made since his days.

Galileo

The earliest of these discoveries had been made by an Italian, Galileo. Born in 1564, he was an independent man, who would not believe things just because everybody else did, but insisted on seeing things and working things out for himself. He was interested in everything to do with science, but really became famous in 1609 when, after looking at the planets through a telescope he had copied from a Dutch design, he announced that all the other scholars had been wrong, and Copernicus was right. The earth, he said, far from being the centre of the universe, actually revolved round the sun. What was more, he was prepared to prove this to anyone who would come and look through his telescope.

Galileo's idea was rejected out of hand by many scholars. Few of them would even bother to look through his telescope. Who was he with his little tube with bits of glass in it to contradict the teachings of scholars for ages past? It was all nonsense, they said. Moreover, it was

Left: from vague rumours of a spyglass invented in Flanders, Galileo constructed this telescope in 1609. (He was the first to use a telescope for looking at the stars.)
Right: some of the observations he made.

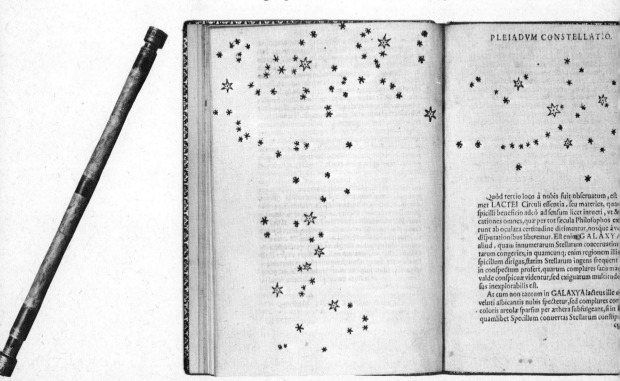

dangerous nonsense, for it went against the teaching of the Church. Many people advised him to keep quiet, but he refused. Indeed, he published his conclusions in a book which was quite unlike any scientific book ever written. For one thing, it was written, not in Latin, but in Italian. This meant that it could be understood by many ordinary people as well as the scholars. In addition, it was written in a lively style which made it interesting to read. The printing presses turned out thousands of copies, and Galileo's theories were soon the talk of northern Italy. At last, in 1616, the Church, thinking that its authority was being undermined, condemned his theory as 'false and altogether opposed to Holy Scripture'. Galileo was then forced to declare in public that in fact the earth was the centre of the universe, and that it stood still. He made his declaration, and from then on his work was supervised by the Church who could, however, do nothing to prevent his theory spreading. Gradually it was accepted by scholars everywhere, and in 1822 the Church at last accepted it too.

Galileo and mechanics

Although Galileo became famous because of his clash with the Church, he did other work as well, in its way just as important. He was fascinated by movement of any sort and tried to find out the rules which govern it.

The ancient Greeks had taught that movement is unnatural. They thought that something only moves so long as some force is either pushing it or pulling it, like a man with a wheelbarrow. When the man stops pushing, the barrow stops moving. Galileo was not happy with this theory. If it was true, then why did an arrow go on moving after it left the bow? What made a ball roll after it left the hand? He never found a completely convincing answer, but he did enough work to show that the old idea was wrong. It was left to Newton to find the real answer, as we shall see.

He did make some important discoveries about movement, however. It was he who, while watching the great lamps swinging to and fro in the cathedral at Pisa, noticed that no matter how far they might swing they always took the same amount of time to get from the one side to the other. He had discovered the principle of the pendulum. By running different weights in trolleys down slopes, he discovered that light objects fall just as fast as heavy ones, which seemed against common sense. What is more, he discovered how to calculate how quickly an object will fall.

The importance of experiments

Most of Galileo's discoveries were made by doing experiments. This was something new. Most scientists believed that the only use of experiments was to illustrate the truths handed down from the Greeks. If an experiment showed that the Greeks were wrong, then something was the matter with either the scientist's apparatus or his reasoning. As a result, experimenters went to all sorts of lengths to try to square up Galileo's conclusion that light objects fall just as quickly as heavy ones with Aristotle's teaching that heavy ones fall faster. They found it impossible to do so. In the end, they preferred the words of Aristotle to the evidence of their own eyes.

Clearly, Galileo himself did not take this view. Nor did Francis Bacon, a famous scholar, who rose to be Lord Chancellor of England. He believed that the best way to learn is to do experiments, and if their results did not agree with the accepted theory then, Bacon argued, the theory was shown to be wrong and a new one would have to be formulated. In this way, he taught, man would go on learning more and more about the world in which he lived. There was no end to the facts he could accumulate and at last all this knowledge might lead to a new view of the universe.

The Royal Society

Fired with Bacon's ideas, a group of British scientists formed a society where they could meet regularly, discuss their ideas, and perform experiments. For seventeen years they worked and discussed at their regular meetings, but in 1662 they really came into the limelight when Charles II granted them a charter, and they became the Royal Society. Charles himself was very interested in science and he and his brother James were both active members of the Royal Society and attended

Sir Francis Bacon.

Bacon's successors liked experiments with a touch of the extraordinary about them. In 1650 a hanged woman, apparently dead, was taken from the scaffold and 'revived' by Dr William Petty, a member of the group which later became the Royal Society.

195

meetings regularly. Charles's support made science fashionable and many of his courtiers joined as well. Pepys was a member, and he records how he attended one meeting where there was a discussion about the comet which had just appeared, and another where Sir George Ent, the President of the Royal College of Physicians, gave a talk on breathing. During this talk Sir George frankly admitted that nobody knew how breathing 'is managed by nature or for what use it is'. On another occasion he attended a gala demonstration put on for the benefit of the Duchess of Newcastle, who was accompanied by Lord George Berkeley, the Earl of Carlisle and the Duke of Somerset. The Duchess was shown experiments with colours, magnets and liquids. Most impressive, a piece of roast mutton was turned into pure blood in her presence. She was, says Pepys, 'full of admiration, all admiration'.

This new Royal Society was very important, because not only did all the leading scientists in London meet and talk over their problems and experiments, but they also printed their transactions so that anybody interested could read them. Soon the Royal Society in England was joined by a similar one in France, and others like them were founded in other countries.

Robert Boyle

An early member of the society was Robert Boyle, the youngest son of the Earl of Cork. He was born in 1627 and spent much of his time doing experiments. He was particularly interested in gases, trying to find out what they are. He discovered that air is a substance which can be weighed, and found out that the volume occupied by a gas decreases in proportion as the pressure increases – a proposition which is still called Boyle's Law. But, even more important, he rejected out of hand the idea that everything is composed of the four elements of fire, water, earth and air, and poured scorn on the idea that one metal could be turned into another. It was his discoveries that made the study of chemistry as we know it today possible.

Isaac Newton

But the most famous member of the Royal Society was Isaac Newton. Born in 1642, he was so small a baby that his mother said he could have been put into a quart pot, but he grew to be one of the greatest scientists who have ever lived. In his early years he was, like Galileo, fascinated by the movement of the planets. Earlier scientists had shown that the planets revolved round the sun not in a circle, but in an ellipse. The questions which concerned Newton were why the planets stayed in the same track, and why they moved at all. He was wondering about this problem one autumn day in the orchard of his home at Woolsthorpe in Lincolnshire, when his attention was distracted by an apple falling from one of the trees. Suddenly an idea occurred to him.

The Greeks had taught that all solids in the universe are attracted to the centre of the earth, but Newton went further than this. Just as the

Portrait of Sir Isaac Newton painted in 1702.

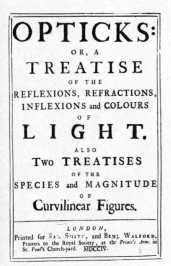

Above: title page of *Opticks*.
Above right: Newton's reflecting
telescope, made in 1668.
The eyepiece is just below
the top of the telescope, with
a mirror inside to reflect the
object. Newton believed that
this would get rid of the
coloured edges to the images.

earth attracted the apple, so the sun might be attracting all the planets.
With this idea in mind, he set to work. After long and complicated
calculations which would have been impossible without recent discoveries in mathematics, such as algebra and logarithms, he was
able to prove that the solar system is held together by a force – he
called it the force of gravity – which the sun and all the planets exert
on each other.

This discovery alone would have been enough to make Newton famous for ever, but it was only a part of his work. Like Galileo, he was
dissatisfied with the Greek idea that an object will only move so long as
some force is pushing it along. In the end he was able to prove that in
fact it will go on moving until something stops it. Thus it was rest, not
movement, that was unnatural. He found out that white light is made
up of a mixture of lights of different colours. In addition, he completely
revolutionized the whole study of mathematics. But the odd thing is that
to Newton these discoveries were not really the most important part of
his work. He often did not bother to publish his discoveries, and, indeed,
frequently lost his notes and calculations, for he was preoccupied with
the study of chemistry and alchemy, seeking a way to change one metal
into another. He worked so long and hard at this that it brought on a
nervous breakdown in 1693, and Newton had to leave Cambridge,
where he had worked up to then and come to London. Once in London,
he soon became President of the Royal Society and Master of the Mint.

PROSPECTUS INTRA CAMERAM STELLATAM.

One of the rooms of
Greenwich Observatory. A
quadrant is in use *(left)* and a
long telescope *(right)*. The
portraits are those of Charles II
and James II.

Halley's comet, photographed
in 1910. Sir Edmund Halley
(1656–1742) gave his name
to this comet by working out
its orbit round the sun and
predicting its return every
seventy-six years. It is due
back in 1986.

Newton's impact

Newton died in 1727. Those who lived and worked with him had no doubt that he was a great genius. No other man has ever made so many basic discoveries and scientists have been building on the foundations he laid ever since. Alexander Pope, a poet who lived at the same time as Newton summed up his achievement in two lines:

Nature and Nature's laws lay hid in night:
God said, 'Let Newton be!' and all was light.

Phlogiston

In the years after Newton's death, the most important discoveries were made by chemists, who were trying to find out exactly what happened when something burned. They came to the conclusion that a mysterious substance was given up in the smoke. They called this substance 'phlogiston'. It was pointed out that when some substances burn, they actually become heavier, but this did not trouble the Phlogistians. They simply replied that this showed that Phlogiston weighed less than nothing. Their theory took a strong hold, and when Joseph Priestley, an English chemist living in Birmingham, heated mercuric oxide and got pure oxygen, he called it 'dephlogisticated air', because it sucked the phlogiston out of things so quickly when they were burned in it. Priestley had his house ransacked because he was thought to approve of the

Some of Priestley's apparatus for experiments with gases. For heat he used either the fire or a candle. The crudity of the apparatus made accurate experiments difficult.

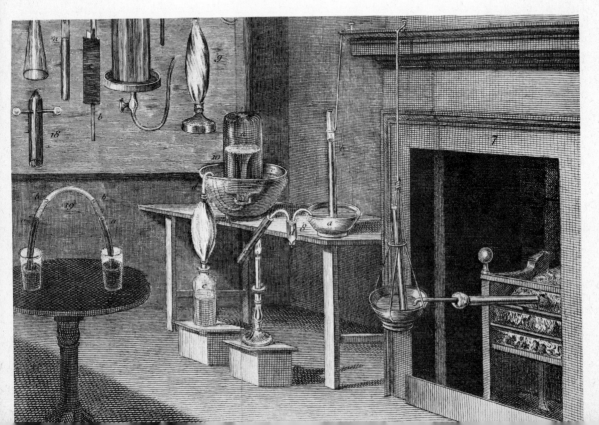

French Revolution, but even he did not fare so badly as the man who finally discovered that in burning, a substance in fact combines with a part of the air, which he called oxygen. This man was Lavoisier, a Frenchman, who was not only a chemist, but also a tax-collector. In 1794 he was guillotined. The revolutionaries in France were not interested in his experiments, only in his tax-gathering.

Scientific instruments

Many of the scientific discoveries would have been impossible without accurately made instruments and apparatuses. The barometer was discovered in the middle of the seventeenth century, and the thermometer a hundred years later. In the Middle Ages, scientific apparatus was heavy and clumsy, but gradually men grew more skilled in precision work. One of these instrument-makers, John Harrison by name, succeeded, in 1759, in designing a watch which only lost five seconds during a voyage to Jamaica. This was an important invention, as it is essential to know the exact time in order to be able to work out the position of a ship at sea. Harrison's invention made it possible for the first time for a captain to pinpoint his position on the ocean, even if there was no land in sight, and it also made it easier to make accurate charts. Harrison did well out of his watch, for he won a prize of £14,000 which the Admiralty had been offering for such a discovery.

Left: Harrison's first chronometer, invented in 1735. *Above:* his fourth model, dating from 1759, measured approximately 5¼ inches in diameter.

The effect of scientific discoveries

It is easy to see what sort of effect an invention has. It is not so easy to see the impact of the discovery of a new scientific law. Yet some of these discoveries were very important for their effect on the lives of thousands of people even at the time. Many of the inventions of the Industrial Revolution depended on the work done by Newton and the other scientists. It is, for instance, impossible to understand the working of the steam engine without knowing Boyle's Law. But, more important, like all advances in science, they laid the foundations on which later scientists could build. The scientists of the day realized this. They prided themselves on their knowledge of the world in which they lived, for they now knew more than the great philosophers of ancient Greece. None the less, the problems which they had solved had left hundreds of further questions unanswered. They hoped that scientists in the future would find the answers and that this increased knowledge would bring in the end a golden age when all men would be happy and contented. They were wrong.

Things to do

1 Try to write a conversation between yourself and a boy or girl of your own age, living in 1600, about science.
2 Try to find out more about some of the discoveries of the scientists mentioned in the chapter.

Books to read

D. C. Knight, *Isaac Newton*, Chatto and Windus.

R. B. Marcus, *Galileo and Experimental Science*, Chatto and Windus.

J. D. North, *Isaac Newton*, Oxford University Press

C. A. Ronan (ed.), *Newton and Gravitation*, Cape (Jackdaw)

F. Sherwood Taylor, *An Illustrated History of Science*, Heinemann Educational.

H. Sootin, *Robert Boyle*, Chatto and Windus.

Chapter 15
Doctors and surgeons

Illness and injury can be frightening things, and it is a great comfort to know that there are physicians who are specially trained to cure us when we fall ill, and surgeons whose job it is to set our bones if we break them, remove organs if they become diseased, and stitch us up again if we gash ourselves open. The result is that doctors are valued and respected members of society – and they always have been, even when their knowledge and skill were not nearly so great as they are today. Even jungle tribes have their witch-doctors, who, even though they have little or no medical knowledge, are still men with great power and influence.

Eighteenth-century physicians

British doctors in the seventeenth and eighteenth centuries had a good deal in common with witch-doctors. This is not to say that they wore odd clothes, painted their faces and danced round their patients muttering spells; indeed, the popular physician dressed in the height of fashion, complete with wig and sword, rode from call to call in his own coach, and walked up to his patients in a very imposing way, supported by a gold-headed cane. No, it is only when we come to look at how much he really knew about disease, and the drugs he used to cure them, that the similarity becomes clear.

In order to practise, physicians had to be licensed by the Royal College of Physicians, set up in 1518, but it only needed a slight knowledge of ancient Greek ideas about medicine to get the licence, especially if you were only going to practise in the provinces. London doctors were expected to be more learned. All that they really knew was that when you were ill, something had happened to upset the normal working of your body. They had no idea of what caused this upset, or of how to put it right. Not that many of them realized this. Indeed, they claimed to have a remedy for every upset.

Diagnosis

But before they knew what to give you, they had to find out what was wrong with you. If he visited you, the doctor would find out if you were feverish by putting his hand on your forehead. He had no thermometer. Then he would ask questions and perhaps squeeze and push a few tender places in the hope of finding out something obviously wrong. And that would be all. He had no stethoscope to listen to what was happening inside, and even if he had, he would not have understood what he heard. So little was learned from such examinations that some doctors would

The Royal College of Physicians in London, as it appeared in 1750.

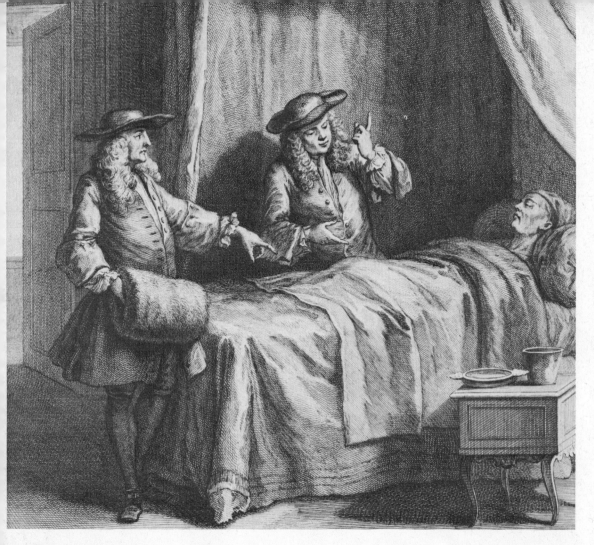

Two physicians at a patient's bedside discussing his condition. If he survives he will have a heavy bill to pay.

prescribe without visiting their patient at all. Others, called water doctors, would simply look at a sample of their patient's urine and diagnose the disease from that – though they probably learned more from the spies they had stationed in the waiting-room than they did from the contents of the little bottles they examined so gravely.

Remedies

But whatever method of diagnosis they used, the doctor would prescribe something to make the patient feel better. Sometimes it would be a draught of medicine to drink, or a pill to swallow. These might contain anything from bone marrow and sweat, to blood and shavings from the skull of an executed criminal, for all these items were on the official list of drugs published in 1618. Otherwise the doctor might order poultices and dressings to be placed on painful places to draw out whatever was causing the pain. For instance, half a newly-killed pigeon was

ALTISSIMVS
CREAVIT DE TERRA MEDECINAM ET VI[...]
PRVDENS NON ABHOREBIT ILLAM
ANNO DOMMINI 1623

A signboard belonging to a seventeenth-century doctor, showing his various accomplishments, including amputations and tooth extractions. The Latin inscription reads: 'The all-highest created medicine from the earth and the prudent man will not despise it.'

thought to do no end of good if placed on plague sores. Most likely of all, he would order some blood to be let. This was thought to be a good thing for almost any disease. Indeed, some people, like Pepys, had blood taken from them regularly even when they felt quite well, just to be on the safe side. Sometimes this blood-letting was done by cutting open a vein with a lancet, but other doctors preferred to use leeches, black slug-like creatures which live on blood. These were put on the patient's skin and would bite him, and suck about half an ounce of blood each before they were full, when they would drop off.

A royal illness

The more serious your disease, or the richer you were, the more doctors would be called and the more remedies tried. When Charles II collapsed in February 1685, he first had blood let and then had pans of hot coal put on his body to try to bring him round. From that moment until his death three days later, the doctors, rarely fewer than four at a time, worked on him day and night. Time after time they gave him laxatives and things to make him vomit. They let blood at regular intervals, they put burning plasters on him to raise blisters, gave him sneezing powders and made lots of little cuts on various parts of his body. For nourishment they allowed him a little thin broth and some light ale. As he grew weaker, they dosed him with quinine and finally, as a last resort, they bled him again. It is no wonder that he died, the treatment might well have killed a man in good health.

Thomas Sydenham, the Puritan physician

Charles might well have got on better if Thomas Sydenham had been looking after him. Born in 1624, he had much better ideas than most doctors of his day. He believed that the only way to learn about diseases was to sit at the patient's bedside and watch carefully, noting all the symptoms. Comparing one case with another, Sydenham found that some showed exactly the same pattern of events as the illness went on. This was a great help to him, for he now knew what to expect to happen next when he met this pattern again, and if he had found that a particular remedy worked before, then he could try it once more in the hope that it might again be successful. His investigations had taught him that in fact few of the usual remedies were of much use. He found that Nature would cure most diseases on her own if given a chance and plenty of fresh air. He discovered and named scarlet fever, and wrote several medical books, which seem now to be much more sensible than any other such works written in the seventeenth century. But his fellow-doctors took little notice of him. He was a Puritan, and therefore unfashionable. They were happiest when using the old remedies in the old way.

A contemporary portrait of Thomas Sydenham.

The doctor's fee

But however ignorant he might be by modern standards, the physician

wanted his fee. Some charged as much as five guineas a visit, in addition to travelling expenses of a guinea a mile. True, they were meant to treat the poor free of charge, and some did so, but many had only time for rich patients and made a great deal of money. For instance, one doctor, Sir Richard Jebb, made 20,000 guineas between 1779 and 1787, and another, Sir Theodore Mayerne, left £140,000 when he died. Both of these men were fashionable London doctors. Country doctors would not make more than a comfortable living, and some had difficulty in even doing that, but, if they were to live at all, they had to charge fees. The result was that a poor man rarely saw a physician. He relied on traditional cures, or called on the apothecary.

A seventeenth-century drug shop. The drugs are kept in bottles and boxes on the shelves, and are mixed with the pestle and mortar by the youth in the centre. (From a French engraving.)

The apothecary and his wares

The apothecary has disappeared from modern life. The nearest thing we have to him is the chemist who makes up the prescription given to us by the doctor. But the apothecary did more than that. It is true that he kept a shop, which was well stocked with all sorts of drugs, but in addition to selling these, he acted as a doctor to the poor. He was not really qualified to do this – his only training was usually to have served an apprenticeship with another apothecary, but his fees were much lower than those of a physician. He made most of his money by selling drugs and patent medicines. This meant that he was sometimes something of a slick salesman, and was looked down on by the respectable. Newspapers of the day carried many advertisements for his wares. For instance, there were:

Grant's incomparable and never failing drops (price one shilling the bottle), a speedy cure for Coughs, Colds, Asthmas, Phthisic, Wheezings, difficult breathing, shortness of breath and all sorts of Consumptions, even when so far advanced as not to be cured by any other Medicine in the World.

If, like John Harris, you had a weak constitution and, in addition, had suffered from 'wind, Cholic and pains in the stomach and bowels, also a very bad digestion and frequent vomiting for upward of sixteen years', you needed only to take one box of Mr Speediman's stomach pills, at one and sixpence the box. These pills 'dispersed the wind in a very surprising manner, quite check'd the vomiting and removed the pain in the stomach and bowels and created a good appetite'. Even if Speediman's pills had not worked, Mr Harris need not have worried. He could always have tried Maredant's Drops, 'never sold for less than Six Shillings the bottle'. These would 'perfect digestion and amazingly create an appetite', in addition to curing 'leprosy, scurvy, ulcers, the evil, fistula, piles, long-continued inflammations of the eyes and every other disorder arising from a foulness in the blood'. If, after all this, he was attacked by 'Agues, intermittent or Nervous Fevers', or 'too lax a state of the fibres', he could have at hand a bottle of Febrifuge Elixir, a new preparation of Peruvian Bark or quinine, certain to cure him. The price was not stated. If some of the claims for these medicines, all advertised in a local newspaper in 1774, seem absurd, then take a look at the advertisements in today's papers.

Cures for the poor

Effective or not, such medicines, widely advertised, sold well and the apothecary cheerfully took the money. Most of his patients recovered, and recommended his cures to their friends. After all, a shilling or two spent on pills was much less than the fee of even the humblest physician. For the really poor, however, even a shilling was too much. When they were ill, they took either nothing, or else relied on traditional remedies handed down from the past. Here are a few of them, current in Hertfordshire in the eighteenth century. To cure jaundice, it was recommended to take nine lice in a little ale every morning for a week. Shingles could be cured by using ointment made up of blood from a black cat's tail, mixed with juice from a house-leek and cream. Ague was relieved either by taking strong beer and honey, or by dumping the sufferer into a tub

An English engraving of an apothecary. He is engaged in sorting out herbs. The stuffed animals hanging from the ceiling were common in such shops.

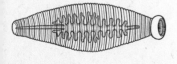

A leech.

of cold water. Hedgehog dripping dropped into the ear was a certain cure for deafness, while consumption could be banished by drinking 'the very disagreeable liquor' produced by boiling turnips with a piece of rusty bacon. Swallowing young frogs was good for asthma and hog's dung would stop bleeding. Oddest of all, rashes and skin diseases could be put right by carrying a dried toad in a silk bag around one's neck. Such were the medicines of the very poor.

The surgeons – Harvey and the bloodstream

In addition to physicians and apothecaries, there were also the surgeons, but they were not nearly so important as physicians. Many of them were simply barbers, who did a bit of blood-letting and bone-setting in their spare time. Henry VIII had granted the Barber Surgeons a charter which had given the company the right to dissect the bodies of four criminals each year. Otherwise dissection was illegal. Many surgeons, therefore, left England to train abroad, where dissection was legal, and it was at Padua, in Italy, that an English surgeon, named William Harvey, discovered that the blood was pumped by the heart all around the body. You might think that people would flock to consult so clever a doctor when he returned to London, but in fact his practice went down after he had published a book about his discovery. People thought he was a crank.

Many experiments were made with blood transfusion in the seventeenth century. Doctors did not realize how many different types of blood there were, and thus made attempts, doomed to failure, to transfer human blood to animals.

The resurrection men

Those surgeons who remained in Britain were at a great disadvantage They either had to learn the details of human anatomy from their own patients – which was often too late – or else break the law by dissecting bodies sold to them by 'resurrection men'. These men would go round to the churchyard the night after a burial, carefully remove all the wreaths, dig up the coffin, take the body, and replace the soil and the wreaths. Nobody would be any the wiser, and a skilled gang could do the whole job in less than an hour, selling the body for as much as three guineas.

This print shows two 'resurrection men' disturbed at their trade by the arrival of a clergyman and a donkey, whose braying frightens them.

Hogarth's view of a dissection. The subject is an executed criminal, with the rope still round his neck. The lecturer uses his pointer to draw his audience's attention to important details as his assistants perform the dissection.

These resurrection men were so unpopular that they ran the risk of being torn to pieces if the mob caught them, and all sorts of things were done to try to stop their activities. Churchyards were surrounded with huge iron railings, with only a small gate, guarded by a watchman. More and more people were buried in huge underground rooms, the entrance to which was sealed by a heavy stone, securely locked in place, but still the thefts continued. At one London churchyard, where they employed a watchman and a dog, the thieves not only took a body, but the dog as well. Matters improved a little after 1745, when the new Company of Surgeons, with its headquarters at Surgeon's Hall, London, was given a regular supply of bodies to dissect, but in some places, notably Edinburgh, where the first medical school for the training of doctors was set up, the demand for bodies was still much greater than the supply of criminals. This meant that the practice went on, and was sometimes winked at by the authorities, who knew that a surgeon needed to practise dissection on dead bodies if he was to be able to operate successfully on live ones.

Operations

Not that surgeons could do many operations. For one thing, they were limited by the length of time that a patient could bear the agony of being cut about without an anaesthetic, and for another, their patients frequently died of blood-poisoning, caused by dirty instruments. As a rule the surgeon had only to be able to set or amputate damaged limbs, let blood and cut for the stone. This was the only major operation performed and involved cutting open the patient and removing a stone which had formed in the bladder or kidney. The pain from such a stone was so great that people would rather undergo the agony and risk of an operation than bear their stone. In the seventeenth century, it could be quite a long operation, and was always very hazardous.

Frère Jacques and William Cheseldon

Many surgeons tried to shorten the operation of cutting for the stone, and in 1697 a French priest – Frère Jacques, began to use a method by which he plunged a knife into his patient's stomach near the hip, worked it up and down to enlarge the wound, and then inserted his fingers and extracted the stone. The whole operation took less than a minute, but many of Jacques' patients only survived long enough to sign a certificate that the operation had been successful. None the less, the Frenchman became famous, and crowds came to watch him operate in theatres up and down the country. Soon his fame spread to England, and in 1727 William Cheseldon modified his method to make it safer, and was soon charging 500 guineas for removing stones, though he always operated on the poor free of charge. His reputation spread all over the country and helped to improve the reputation of surgeons in general, though they were still not in the same class as physicians.

John Hunter

The man who did most for surgery in the eighteenth century was John Hunter. He realized that the key to good surgery was not only speed and accuracy. These were important, but far more vital was a complete knowledge of exactly what lay under the skin of the human body. He wanted to find out the shape and function of every human organ. To gain this knowledge, Hunter dissected not only human bodies, but also every sort of animal he could lay his hands on. By the time he died, it was reckoned he had dissected over 500 different types of animal and well over 3,000 human bodies. The knowledge that he gained from the comparisons he was able to make between one body and another, and one animal and another, provided the necessary information to make surgery a science, though it was not until the discovery, described in *A History of Britain*, SH4, of anaesthetics and antiseptics a hundred years later that operations began to be safe and successful.

Eighteenth-century lancets. The blade folds into the handle rather like a penknife. One has a steel blade, the other has one made of ivory and was used for vaccinations.

John Hunter, painted in his study by Reynolds.

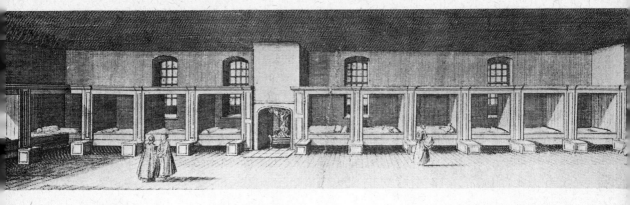

A ward in Guy's Hospital. Notice the small number of windows and their size.

The age of hospitals

Another great step forward in medicine in the eighteenth century was the founding of hospitals. There had been hospitals in the Middle Ages, but these had been places where people had gone to be taken care of rather than to be cured. Most of these hospitals had disappeared at the Dissolution of the Monasteries – only three survived in London, St Thomas's, St Bartholomew's and St Mary's. Now, between 1720 and 1745, four more were founded. These hospitals provided wonderful centres for training. Here students could actually watch the great physician or surgeon at work on a patient, and compare one case with another. What was more, if there was a particularly sensational operation, they could even invite their friends into the theatre to watch. In such places, though they were often dirty and insanitary, and the nurses usually completely untrained and ignorant, much could be learned by young physicians and surgeons. Gradually, then, doctors grew more learned and skilled, but the greatest advances were not really made until the nineteenth century.

A 1720 print of St Bartholomew's hospital in Smithfield.

Bedlam

There have always been some members of society whose minds have been in such a state that it has been impossible for them to live normal lives. It is only within the last century that doctors have begun to understand how to treat such people so that they can recover and lead a normal life. Two hundred and fifty years ago, they were simply labelled 'lunatics', and shut up in hospital so that they could do no harm. The most famous hospital for lunatics was that of St Mary of Bethlehem, or as it was usually known, 'Bedlam', in London. This hospital, founded in the Middle Ages, was one of the sights of London. For a penny visitors could go round the galleries, peering into the cells at the patients, provoking and teasing them into transports of rage, for their amusement. In 1770, after many protests, this 'penny visiting' was stopped and it was laid down that all visitors had to be accompanied by an attendant. Conditions in Bedlam had so distressed some doctors, however, that

Bedlam, by Hogarth. A new arrival is put into irons, while two fashionable ladies tour the hospital. One patient thinks he is Pope, another imagines himself to be king.

they founded another similar hospital in London, called St Luke's. This was rather better run, and provided a pattern which was copied in other hospitals founded up and down the country in the years which followed.

Treatment

Once inside a hospital like Bedlam, the unfortunate patient might be subjected to the most frightful treatment. One seventeenth-century doctor wrote:

Nothing is more necessary and more effective for the recovery of these people than forcing them to respect and fear intimidation. This is why maniacs often recover much sooner if they are treated with torture and treatment in hovels instead of with medicaments.

It was usual for violent patients to be kept permanently in chains, and others had their blood let, were given vomits and laxatives, were kept drugged with opium, or were dumped into baths of cold water. It was rare for patients to be cured. Indeed, they frequently tended to get worse.

Private hospitals

Apart from the big public hospitals, there were also private asylums, run for profit. A few were efficient and well organized, but others were shocking. Some of them would even take in and imprison sane people, whose relatives wanted to get them out of the way, while others took in many more patients than they could possibly care for, simply to get more money. In 1763 a committee of the House of Commons was appointed to inquire into such places, and they recommended that an act should be passed to regulate them. In 1774 such an act became law, but it was so vague that it had little effect, and the treatment of 'lunatics' continued to be cruel and unenlightened.

The hospital for children abandoned by their parents. Such institutions were entirely supported by charity.

Abortive and Stilborne—	617	Executed ———	21	Palsie ———	30
Aged———	1545	Flox and Smal Pox———	655	Plague ———	68596
Ague and Feaver ———	5257	Found dead in streets, fields, &c.	20	Plannet ———	6
Appoplex and Suddenly———	116	French Pox———	86	Plurisie ———	15
Bedrid ———	10	Frighted ———	23	Poysoned ———	1
Blasted———	5	Gout and Sciatica ———	27	Quinsie ———	35
Bleeding———	16	Grief———	46	Rickets ———	557
Bloudy Flux, Scowring & Flux	185	Griping in the Guts———	1288	Rising of the Lights———	397
Burnt and Scalded———	8	Hangd & made away themselves	7	Rupture ———	34
Calenture ———	3	Headmouldshot & Mouldfallen	14	Scurvy———	105
Cancer, Gangrene and Fistula-	56	Jaundies ———	110	Shingles and Swine pox———	2
Canker, and Thrush———	111	Imposthume———	227	Sores, Ulcers, broken and bruised	
Childbed———	625	Kild by several accidents———	46	Limbes ———	82
Chrisomes and Infants———	1258	Kings Evill———	86	Spleen ———	14
Cold and Cough ———	68	Leprosie———	2	Spotted Feaver and Purples	1929
Collick and Winde———	134	Lethargy———	14	Stopping of the Stomack—	332
Consumption and Tissick —	4808	Livergrowne ———	20	Stone and Strangury ———	98
Convulsion and Mother —	2036	Meagrom and Headach———	12	Surfet———	1251
Distracted———	5	Measles———	7	Teeth and Worms———	2614
Dropsie and Timpany———	1478	Murthered, and Shot———	9	Vomiting ———	51
Drowned ———	50	Overlaid and Starved———	45	Wenn———	1

	Males—— 5114			Males—— 48569		
Christned	Females— 4853		Buried	Females— 48737	Of the Plague—	68596
	In all—— 9967			In all—— 97306		

Increased in the Burials in the 130 Parishes and at the Pest-house this year——— 79009
Increased of the Plague in the 130 Parishes and at the Pest-house this year——— 68590

Things to do

1 Look at the Bill of Mortality for 1665 above. Try to find out the modern names of as many of the diseases as you can.

2 Find out how long a surgeon has to train today and what sort of examinations he has to sit. Compare these to that described in the following extract.

It comes from a novel called *Roderick Random*, written in 1748. Smollett, who wrote it, knew what he was talking about, as he was a surgeon himself.

I was conducted into a large hall, where I saw about a dozen of grim faces sitting at a long table; one of whom bade me come forward in such an imperious tone that I was actually for a minute or two bereft of my senses. He then proceeded to interrogate me about my age, the town where I had served my time, with the term of my apprenticeship; and when I informed him that I had served three years only, he fell into a violent passion: (and) swore it was a shame and a scandal to send such raw boys into the world as surgeons. This reduced me to such a situation that I was scarce able to stand. A plump gentleman who sat opposite to me with a skull before him, examined me touching the operation of the trepan, and was very well satisfied with my answers. The next person who questioned me was a wag,

The Bill of Mortality for London in 1665. Perhaps the oddest cause of death entered is 'Plannet', which means that it was caused by the influence of the stars. Before we sneer, remember how many people today still read their horoscopes.

who began by asking if I had ever seen amputation performed; and I replying in the affirmative, he shook his head, and said, 'What! upon a dead subject I suppose?' 'Suppose you was called to a patient of a plethoric habit, who been bruised by a fall, what would you do?' I answered I would bleed him immediately. 'What,' said he, 'before you had tied up his arm?' But this stroke of wit not answering his expectation, he desired me to advance to the gentleman who sat next to him, who with a pert air, asked what method of cure I would follow in wounds of the intestines. I repeated the method of cure as it is prescribed by the best chirurgical writers; which he heard to an end, and then said, with a supercilious smile, 'So you think by such treatment the patient might recover? Did you ever know of a case of this kind succeed?' I answered that I did not, and was about to tell him I had never seen a wounded intestine; but he stopped me by saying, with some precipitation 'Nor never will. I affirm that all wounds of the intestines, whether great or small, are mortal.' 'Pardon me, brother,' says the fat gentleman, 'there is very good authority –' Here he was interrupted by the other (and) all the examiners espoused the opinion of one or other of the disputants, and raised their voices all together, when the chairman commanded silence, and ordered me to withdraw. In less than a quarter of an hour I was called in again, received my qualification sealed up, and was ordered to pay five shillings.

3   Find out any 'traditional cures' still in use.
4   Make a list of the hospitals in your own town or district. Find out when they were founded.

Books to read

M. Goaman, *Thomas Guy*, Macmillan

John Hawke-Genn, *A Doctor at the Time of the Plague*, Oxford University Press

R. B. Marcus, *William Harvey*, Chatto and Windus

J. Miller (ed.), *Harvey and the Circulation of the Blood*, Cape (Jackdaw)

Index

Numbers listed in italics (e.g. *15*) refer to the captions of illustrations and maps. fl. *stands for* flourished.

Acknowledgements

ILLUSTRATION ACKNOWLEDGEMENTS

Abelard-Schuman Ltd, Peter Mathias, *English Trade Tokens*, photo
 A. C. Barrington-Brown : 181
Archive Teaching Units, University of Sheffield Institute of Education:
 167
British Museum : 11, 12, 13, 27, 28, 36/37, 38, 41, 44, 46, 48, 50,
 52, 55, 60, 61, 68, 76/77, 78, 83, 87, 89, 91, 93, 96, 112, 113, 118,
 130, 131, 135, 136, 139, 143, 144, 145, 146, 147, 165, 166, 178,
 185, 186, 193, 209. Photographs John Webb: 16, 30, 53, 62, 72,
 73, 104, 105, 117, 141
Clarendon Press, Oxford, Purver & Bohen: *The Beginning of the Royal
 Society* : 195
Alex C. Cowper, photographer : 107
John R. Freeman (Photographers) Ltd : 150, 151
Mr Kevis of Petworth, photographer : 155
Leicestershire County Council: 162
London Museum : 137
The Lord Chamberlain : 21
Mansell Collection : 9, 24, 39, 57, 59, 62, 65, 66, 67, 90, 102/103,
 108, 110, 114, 123, 143, 158, 169, 189
National Gallery of Canada, Ottawa : 149
National Maritime Museum, Greenwich : 71, 121, 200
National Maritime Museum, Greenwich Hospital: 126
National Portrait Gallery : 7, 18, 22, 43, 54, 58, 69, 70, 76, 99, 111,
 133, 138, 148, 159, 195, 196
Northampton Museums : 142
Parker Gallery, London : 98
Rothamsted Experimental Station : 160
Royal Commission on Historical Monuments (England) : 85, 164
Science Museum : 97, 159, 171, 172, 173, 177, 179, 180, 191, 193,
 197, 198, 199, 200
Society of Antiquaries : 51, 82, 84, 86, 115, 119
Will F. Taylor, photographer : 154
United States Information Service : 125
Victoria and Albert Museum : 56, 122, 132
Wellcome Trust : 202, 203, 204, 205, 206, 207, 208, 210, 211, 212, 213

TEXT ACKNOWLEDGEMENTS

Mr Christopher Hibbert, quotation from *King Mob* :146/7
Monmouthshire Local History Council, *Presenting Monmouthshire* :
 150/1

ARTISTS' CREDITS

Dougald Macdougall : 79, 100
Edward Poulton : 182
Penguin Education Art Department: 8, 17, 19, 29, 33, 34, 35, 42,
 63, 64, 86, 94, 96, 100, 101, 105, 109, 116, 120, 123, 124, 126, 157,
 161, 163, 170, 186, 187, 190, 192